Advance Prai

"This book is for all who have felt annoyed at God's slowness in ending our world's pain and at God permitting the innocent to suffer. Paige Chargois's tough personal struggles prod her to revisit Job's paradigmatic faith amidst serial misfortunes. Her scholarly and stimulating probing suggests that more than mere belief, faith is a courageous act, a stand we may take, with God's grace, when afflicted by disappointment or sadness." **—Rajmohan Gandhi, historian and grandson of Mahatma Gandhi**

"I have been honored to have the Reverend Paige not only as a mentor but also as a friend.

"Join her in this spiritual journey as she delves into the book of Job from a new perspective. She has immersed herself into his life of grief and agony and has emerged from the ash heap with a prophetic need for lamenting in our lives and within the church. Inspiring and thought-provoking, *Living a Job Faith* leaves her readers with a renewed commitment to faith in God and trust in his will." **—Rebecca Holzer**

"Rev. Paige Chargois takes readers on a skillful journey through the book of Job from various perspectives, examining Job's experience from biblical, historical, cultural, literary, theological, and contemporary contexts. The book is fit ammunition for our faith arsenal as we search for answers amid suffering. Through eleven chapters, she wrestles with the text as thoroughly as Job himself wrestles through the forty-two chapters of his story. As Job experienced God in a new way at the end of his trials, so readers will experience God in a new way through the author's thoughtful analysis." **—Rev. Olivia M. Cloud, Author, Associate Editor, R.H. Boyd Publishing, Assistant Pastor, Berean Baptist Church, Nashville, TN**

"Healing through trauma is a process; it is also a spiritual journey. As a licensed therapist, I endorse this book for those seeking to understand a spiritual process for healing through adversity. This manuscript is no ordinary rendition of a known, ancient story but a fresh re-look with new insights that challenge outdated assumptions. Reverend Dr. Paige Chargois, with concise perception, expertly escorts us through Job's spiritual pilgrimage from transactional religion toward personal faith. Her itinerary begins with Job's origin story, contextualized in a Divine Courtroom. On the tour, she directs readers' attention to best and worst practices for comforting the afflicted, and discovering the miseducation of the woman partnered with Job is a key attraction. Offered as an enlightened rebuke, readers are called to re-understand and re-narrate her story. Paige points out the necessity of existential questions when facing calamity, as shifting from "why me?" to "why not me?" can move the wounded toward spiritual growth and earthly purpose. She walks sojourners through a mental reset–suffering as a normative part of human existence–and provides assurance, through the narrative, of adversity's redemptive power. A seasoned guide, Chargois spotlights experiences from her own life that connect to essential lessons in the text, and she offers readers practical gifts of wisdom. Most keenly, her spiritual tour through Job's story shows readers that God often answers one's questions of God with questions of God's own toward a key aim: to uncover truths about self that help one "see" God newly, relationally, experientially, personally, and more deeply. Concluding the tour, Chargois suggests the Book of Job invites readers to consider God as the source of wisdom and to embrace and integrate the Almighty's steadfast love and faithfulness; doing so can help one find meaning and purpose in daily living and relationships. Let the healing begin." **—Stephanie Jacobs, PhD, LMFT, Exhortations, LLC | exhortationswithdrjacobs.com**

"If there was ever a time to become reacquainted with Job's ancient but timeless wisdom, it is now. As we wrestle with what it means for us to be persons and communities of faith in our post-pandemic environment, Dr. Chargois invites us to move with her through Job's journey of crisis and spiritual maturation, undeserved suffering, and loss towards a transformed relationship with God, ourselves, and all of creation. In this well-researched and provocative commentary Dr. Chargois offers a refreshing and invigorating perspective grounded in Biblical scholarship, theological reflection, contemporary psychology, and personal memoir. She explores the difference between a transactional relationship with God and a relationship grounded in intimacy, reverence, mutual engagement, and lived experience. Her writing exhibits a rare gift for articulating the human experience and the divine-human relationship in terms that are accessible, practical, and enlivened with personal warmth." **—Rev. Amelie A. Wimer, Rector, Historic St. John's Episcopal Church, Richmond, VA**

"In *Living a Job Faith: From Tried to Triumphant*, Paige Chargois deals with one of life's great questions: How can a loving God tolerate human suffering? The story of Job highlights the human struggle to find a relationship with a God who often appears distant and unconcerned. Chargois is a scholar, an ordained Christian minister, and a Civil Rights warrior who has worked for international organizations to promote peace and reconciliation. On a personal level, the book helps Chargois come to terms with suffering, injustice, and shame in her own life. The book is an invitation to a spiritual journey that leads from anger, bitterness, and despair to a profound faith in God. Her focus on the prayer of lament offers the reader a way to confront God with our deepest fears and frustrations. The process takes time. If we invest ourselves in self-examination, we eventually arrive at a place of more mature faith. This initiating is important for individuals, and it is also important for the church. As questions about life and faith take us deeper, there is great potential for personal transformation of the church. The practical questions at the end of each chapter are a great help. May Paige's words take us to a place of deep spiritual affirmation." **—Rev. Canon Robert G. Hetherington, Rector Emeritus, St. Paul's Episcopal Church, Richmond, VA**

LIVING A Job FAITH

From Tried to Triumphant

PAIGE LANIER CHARGOIS

Foreword by Patricia Gould-Champ

Judson Press™
DISTINGUISHED PUBLISHERS SINCE 1824
VALLEY FORGE, PA

Living a Job Faith: From Tried to Triumphant

Interior design by Crystal Devine.
Cover design by Anthony Aranha.

Library of Congress Cataloging-in-Publication Data

Names: Chargois, Paige Lanier, 1944- author.
Title: Living a job faith : from tried to triumphant / Paige Chargois.
Identifiers: LCCN 2023030116 (print) | LCCN 2023030117 (ebook) | ISBN 9780817018405 (paperback) | ISBN 9780817082499 (epub)
Subjects: LCSH: Bible. Job--Criticism, interpretation, etc.
Classification: LCC BS1415.2 .C55 2023 (print) | LCC BS1415.2 (ebook) | DDC 223/.106--dc23/eng/20231002
LC record available at https://lccn.loc.gov/2023030116
LC ebook record available at https://lccn.loc.gov/2023030117

Cataloging-in-Publication Data available upon request. Contact cip@judsonpress.com.

Printed in the U.S.A.
First printing, 2024.

Being human is an exceptional journey

that billions of others have already taken

which makes none of us exceptional.

Like Job, it is a journey through that human trauma to
faith in a God who not only answers our questions with
questions of his own

but who can—in our time of need—come to us

in the might and mystery of a whirlwind

to end our languishing on an ash heap

until we can see God for ourselves!

That is the Job story. That is our story.

In the beauty and sometimes traumatic

moments of our human experiences,

I dedicate this literary journey to you.

Let us journey with Job and with one another,

to a new level of faith in which—like Job—we, too,

can move beyond just hearing about God

to seeing God

via the uniqueness of our own personal experience!

To that endeavor, I dedicate this book to you.

CONTENTS

FOREWORD

Living a Job Faith: From Tried to Triumphant is an awesome resource for the soul of every believer! As believers, we live in a world where *faith* is the order of the day. Our faith becomes our badge of honor and an expected power shield that protects us from all life's pain and sorrow. But if the truth be told, in this pandemic-impacted season where the world seems upside down, we often find ourselves individually and collectively as believers in a faith crisis. Our loud but unspoken questions seem to be: where is God in all of this? When I am hurting, how do I remain faithful to a God who appears absent or nonresponsive in my time of need? In times like these, believers need to be lovingly ushered back to a faith that sustains our weary souls and reinforces our relationship with God. I am excited that, as a minister and committed servant who deeply loves the church, Dr. Paige Lanier Chargois has been paying attention to those needs and offers her best work to date to assist her fellow believers in doing just that.

Using the Hebrew Bible story of Job, which mirrors every believer's frustration, Chargois offers a powerful experience that is both timely and needful. By inviting us into an honest and transparent conversation, she allows us to experience God by moving from what we think we know about God and what we have heard about God to finally experiencing and encountering God anew for ourselves. In this season of reimagining and rethinking our faith, this examination becomes critical for those who need to reexamine and reconcile our relationship with a God whom we feel unable to trace, understand, or see. She captures every believer's spiritual frustration in the story of Job and uses his struggle to assist us in our time of struggle when we feel alone and alienated from God.

Living a Job Faith: From Tried to Triumphant invites us into a soul conversation with God. Because where we enter the conversation directs how the conversation will go, she invites us to the conversation at the beginning. She offers us an opportunity to wrestle spiritually and emotionally as believers and to grow in faith from *doing* to *being*. And as we struggle, we move from *tried to triumphant*. We have such a great need for honest dialogue, authentic transparency, and committed wrestling during this season when many are facing some of the darkest moments of their lives. We need a word of hope—something to encourage us to be who we say we are as people of faith. Often, when we find ourselves amid life's pain and sorrow, we declare that we want to have the faith of Job. Well, Chargois helps to unpack what that desire really means. She offers us Biblical clarity, spiritual understanding, and a transformative challenge.

No one can guide and usher us through such a powerful examination of faith as Chargois does. Aside from being a brilliant and gifted writer, she brings to this enterprise a life of faith and service to God and God's people. Her walk of faith is legendary, and her scholarly research of the Book of Job has been recognized and applauded through her doctoral work, as well as through her awesomely prophetic preaching, teaching, and ministry in the church. She is a renowned Old Testament scholar who skillfully combines her personal testimony and anointing as a minister and priest to guide this experience. Her treatment of the Book of Job is an experience like no other. It requires full attention and a release of self to the transformative power of what she shares. Her gifts of research, teaching, and preaching converge to give us a spiritual resource unparalleled by any examination of the life of Job to date.

Several unique and special elements of *Living a Job Faith: From Tried to Triumphant* set it apart from other treatments of the Job story. She is intentional in moving the reader from struggle to triumph. She does not leave us in the state but allows us to experience the struggle and relate it to our lives using well-crafted end-of-chapter questions for reflection and response that draw us in as participants and not just readers. Traditional trigger words like theodicy, evil, and sin are powerfully unpacked and reintroduced to allow us to gain new life-giving inspiration to enhance our relationship with God. Her treatment of Job's wife is especially powerful and freeing for both women and men. Using her knowledge of the Hebrew language, Chargois helps us to understand how past mismanagement and misunderstanding of words can demonize people, cripple our own faith walk, and limit our understanding of God. She is especially adept at helping us reclaim the value of silence during our moments of despair and helps us to receive the wisdom found in those sacred moments.

This book challenges us! Chargois's treatment of the common question of faith during times of trouble (*why me?*) is particularly effective. Through her scholarly examination of Job's story, she moves us from *why me?* to *why not me?* Her thorough examination of the conversations between Job and his friends leads to a profound and useful examination of how *othering* is used as a weapon against suffering people. Her final powerful call to the church and community to return to lament, forgiveness, and reconciliation is unparalleled in this treatment of Job. Understanding that faith is both personal and communal, as a skilled pastor, she lovingly moves the conversation from the individual to the community of faith. Her *Job paradigm* is a definitive pattern and process for spiritual growth, especially during times of crisis.

Chargois's ministry is needed by the church, individually and collectively. Those who struggle to move from "tried to triumphant" especially need her ministry. As she lovingly shares insights that encourage our faith and move us beyond the traditional and mismanaged concepts of faith that devastate us when God does not seem to grant us the results we seek, she challenges us to understand that victory is in the process. Victory is in the questions we ask, the questions we allow to be asked, and the questions God asks of us. This book helps us to experience what we know: the way out is through.

This is a practical book for both the academy and the church. It can guide church groups as they renew their personal relationship with a God who is faithful even in the most troubling times. What a powerful Bible Study resource for churches in transition as churches use the end-of-chapter reflection and response questions to engage in the required dialogue needed for change to take place. As an Associate Professor of Practical Theology, I recommend the use of this book by the academy as it prepares women and men to guide those whom they serve into developing genuine relationships with God and with one another. For those seeking to move beyond a faith that folds at every sign of trouble, this is the book you have been waiting for!

Chargois has not held back; she has given her best scholarship and her best testimony to enhance the faith of the faithful. Realizing the present crisis of faith in the face of these turbulent times, Chargois would not want us to be uninformed or uninspired. She has leased her gift to the body of Christ as a gift from one traveler to another to reassure us that God is with us. The honesty and transparency of over six decades of walking with God are beneficial to those of us who need to follow Job's example of moving from tried to triumphant. Like a caring pastor, Chargois allows us time to reflect, wrestle, and deal with the range of emotions needed to bring about the transformation of faith we need. She artfully and skillfully provides a resource full of insight and inspiration to encourage us to truly walk by faith and connect to God, who promises to never leave nor forsake us, despite what life throws at us daily. I believe that because of this work, the church will be made stronger, and many persons will be spiritually healed and restored to the body of Christ. This is an awesome love gift that ushers the faithful believers, individually and collectively, into a new era of *Living a Job Faith: From Tried to Triumphant!* As we accept this challenge and open ourselves to a continuous transformative encounter with God, we are eternally grateful to Dr. Paige Lanier Chargois!

PATRICIA GOULD-CHAMP, EdD
Associate professor of Practical Theology
Samuel DeWitt Proctor School of Theology,
Virginia Union University

INTRODUCTION

ON OUR EARTH-BOUND JOURNEY, we experience God as alternatively present or absent, depending on various circumstances that come our way. Especially when we suffer sickness, broken trust, financial setbacks, loss of family, or loss of a job, we not only ask, "Why me?" but often ask, "Where is God?" Glance back over the last few years of your life and reflect on times when you may have asked either question. What answers did you receive? What brought you through those soul-anguishing moments?

Just when we think we know God, such traumatizing experiences might quickly make us evaluate what we think we know. The most traumatic season for me was when I realized, after barely five years of marriage, that divorce was practically assured! What compounded that anguish, ushering in shame and a sense of failure, was the reality that it was the first divorce on either side of my very large family of more than fifteen aunts and uncles plus scads of cousins. My husband and I tried and struggled, yet failed six years later. The many wonderful yesterdays we shared were insufficient to secure any successful tomorrows for us. Our only path forward was a divided one, no longer bonded by holy matrimony. Those traumatic years of relational struggle taught me more about my relationship with God than any series of Bible studies or sermons. My faith journey had taught me—and the Book of Job reminds me—that God doesn't allow us to live in our yesterdays but is always crafting a new and better tomorrow for us.

Regardless of how we might qualify God's actions in our lives, God has a way of getting our attention. Suffering can force us to wrap ourselves around that pain while God is calling us to Godself and reassuring us of God's presence. As with Job, once God arrives on the scene, God reassures us of God's ability to make life meaningful and productive once again. What God did for Job, God did for me! And that is what God can do for you!

Have the trust and confidence you poured into others been broken? Perhaps that ushered in the reality that they may have been the wrong recipients of that trust and confidence. We need each other desperately, but such desperation can lead us to mistakenly place more trust and confidence in folks than they deserve. So, what are your choices? To wish you were never born? To curse the moment you were conceived? To instruct God to cross your day of birth off the calendar and never hear "happy birthday" again? A thousand times, no.

It may seem that your trouble, heartache, and pain can move you beyond God's wise and loving reach. But that never happens. Has such pain brought you to the brink of despair or forced you to wonder why you were even born? Join the club. But God never wonders that. God knows the grand purpose for which God gave you life! Is our pain purposeless? Perhaps our troubles, regrets, or sorrows offer us pathways to a grander purpose than what we've yet realized or ever imagined. Can you imagine that your mistakes might have the potential to launch you toward a greater sense of purpose? Can the dangers in which you find yourself create the new music to which you learn to dance your way into a new life? Job survived his trauma; so did I, and you can also. Let Job show you how it's done: ask God to answer your call, ask God to validate your worth, then wait—*even impatiently*—for your darkness to become light!

On the face of it, the biblical story of Job might very well seem allegorical because few, if any, of us have ever encountered someone who has experienced such large-scale serial calamities. You probably know someone whose life has been hit with a series of downfalls that made you exclaim, "They just can't seem to catch a break!" That's Job. Job was a man of stellar reputation within his community. Because of his wealth and the depth of his care for the community, he was highly esteemed. The Hebrew concept of *tzedakah*, meaning charity and justice, is expected of those believed to be righteous. Job clearly defines himself this way: "I hold fast my righteousness, and will not let it go; my heart does not reproach me for any of my days" (Job 27:6, RSV).

Because of the homage afforded him at the city gate, Job might have been regarded as the unofficial "mayor" of his town. Relative to the wealth he attained, he could perhaps be likened to a Jeff Bezos in our day—rich but with a strong sense of benevolence and generosity! To the best of his ability and understanding, Job faithfully served the God in whom he believed with rites and daily sacrifices. For this reason, we can define him as being very devout.

The Book of Job probes the physical, psychological, and spiritual depths of Job's undeserved suffering and allows us to vicariously experience it. Given the episodes of this one man, we are privileged with insight into the profound stress his personal suffering places on his sense of self. The unveiling of Job's story thrusts us into the debate about whether riches and success result from our own righteous behavior or, on the contrary, if God has a different metric for when, how, and with what he chooses to bless or reward any human.

The Book of Job is a biblical example of innocent suffering. The profound anguish Job experiences and speaks to reflects his belief that he has done no wrong. This is exactly what becomes the issue between him and his friends, who cannot accept from Job any assertion that such tragedies could intrude upon an innocent man's life. Their extended conversations with Job about his "hidden" sins and Job's profuse denials comprise the bulk of the book. The Very Rev. Samuel Candler, dean of the Cathedral of Saint Philip, gave the following reason for why the book was included in the Bible: "There is a reason, an important reason, that the Book of Job is (even) in the Bible: because the authentic community of faith, in this case, the Hebrew community of faith, acknowledges that innocent suffering does exist. Job represents innocent suffering. That suffering is authentic because it is not covered up, or solved, or answered, or tidied up, at the end."[1]

Job is us. We are Job. Biblical scholars hail Job as a universal book because it speaks beyond one's religion; it transcends culture, class, and nationality. The Book of Job probes the very depths of our humanity relative to our relationship with God the Creator. It is not a battle of the wills; rather, it is a quest for a greater divine relationship with more than two hundred questions hurled between Job and God. Theologian Tokunboh Adeyemo reminds us "to take the opening chapters seriously, [for] God is the central character, not Job, and the theme of the book is faith, not suffering."[2]

From the earliest Christian systematic interpreters of the Book of Job, such as Clement of Alexandria (c. 150–c. 215) and Origen (c. 185–c. 253), to John Chrysostom (347–407), to contemporary theologians, Job is heralded as the classic example of humans wrestling with self, with family, with friends, and even with God. Theologian Thomas Oden wrote, "In general, we notice that all the works on Job were composed when there existed a contrast between the Alexandrian trend, which interpreted the texts of the Bible by making large use of allegory and the Antiochian trend, which gave preference to a literal interpretation."[3]

Inherent within the book is what Professor E. Glenn Hinson describes as "the synthesis of knowing God and knowing self. If man is without knowledge of God, he is without knowledge of self. Without knowledge of either, he cannot ascertain whether he is a dying life or a living death."[4] Beyond various human crises, the Book of Job presents a journey of faith. This biblical book within the wisdom tradition takes us on the journey from merely having heard about God to finally seeing God in ways that only God can reveal to us. Such a well-defined literary journey as presented in Job helps us discern the difference between the faithful practice of religion and a faith that spiritually enriches every area of our lives. Most people only know of Job's crises and suffering or are aware of him as a man of faith, but few know him as an activist, which Hinson's statement surely implies.

Hinson also writes, "Job not only shunned evil, but he was also committed to obeying the will of God above all else. God twice repeats this description of Job's sterling character (Job 1:8; 2:3), showing that he regards Job as the best representative of his purpose for (humans) on earth."[5] As you read the Book of Job, you will be helped to better distinguish between the powers of good and evil. Reading it will also help you wrestle with and more deeply fathom the concepts of light and darkness and their powerful impact on our daily lives.

Certainly, like individuals, the church is being tried on many fronts and, in the process, is being transformed. I believe that, like Job, the church will also prove itself *triumphant*! Can the Job story be a challenge to the church today? With the loss of millions of active members across the United States, the COVID-19 pandemic forced even the most loyal members into isolation. It's as if some are sitting on their ash heaps of despair, wondering what's happening to the church. Many of us wondered if the church was being forced to find new answers to its old dilemmas of fellowship, faithfulness, finance, missions, and community. Most of us had never heard of the term *Zoom* until the onset of the COVID lockdowns. Zoom changed and transformed many church functions. Churches and worshippers enjoyed worshipping and serving in capacities not previously envisioned. Although some pews remain empty, many believers are content to worship at a distance through the power of technology. Some congregations have not fully rebounded, while others have excelled financially and in memberships—both present and distanced via Zoom. We must diligently lengthen our outreach, proving that the church still cares and is still viable.

The church perhaps could be likened to the primordial pastoral moment for Job in the visit of his three wanna-be theologically astute friends seeking to comfort him; instead, they question his beliefs, undermine his integrity, and doubt the quality of relationship he professes to have with God. Within these contemporary moments, perhaps the church's "three friends" can be identified as the politicians who disdain it, the priests and preachers who abuse it, and some prophets who almost want to pronounce its doom. But more critically, perhaps these friends are like some parishioners who are slow to return to what the church once was pre-pandemic.

Could this be the church's season of agonizing questions, including debates about its quality of worship or sermons tainted with more politics than praise? Perhaps God is calling the church through our contemporary Job-like experience to forgive our social, racial, and political adversaries who have effectively demeaned and diminished the power and place of the church in the life of our nation. We have *othered* them. Will the church experience spiritual renewal, fresh vision, and a deeper commitment to what Christ has called the church to *be*, not just to do?

Does anything in the Book of Job help us perceive how to shake off or be healed of the maladies of the past to serve God better by being made whole again? Nahum Glatzer, University of Frankfurt's chair of Jewish philosophy and ethics, posited that the Book of Job "does not explicitly answer the question it unmistakably asks. It forces one to answer for oneself and therefore to reexamine what one has previously believed about God and man, the nature of good and evil."[6]

The Book of Job, perhaps like no other book, forces us to ask, "Why do we love and serve God? Is it because of our anticipated blessings? Is it because of the good that's present in our lives? Is our relationship that is supposed to be spiritual merely religiously transactional? Does it result from our treasured traditions or our perceived religious duties or obligations?" Satan bluntly queries such questions about Job in his conversation with God. Such conversations—or trials—with Job in absentia tend to change one's perspective about Satan as readers learn that they are not his target. No human is. Rather, the kingdom of God is! Satan's aim is the overthrow of God's kingdom. He intends to de-create all possible aspects of God's incredible creation! The fight is between God and Satan—not between Job, or us, and Satan. God is not oblivious to nor detached from the misfortune we experience! "Elohim calls his handiwork 'good.' . . . The Hebrews often relate descriptions to functionality. When Elohim looked at his handiwork, he did not see that it was 'good,' he saw that it was functional—like a well-oiled and tuned machine."[7] Therefore, Job is functioning as he ought from the Creator's point of view. "Good" is not so much a commendation of Job's behavior as it is a validation of who we are as part of that evident creation.

We know why we marry or seek a certain profession or even choose to become parents, but shouldn't we at times ask ourselves, "Why do I serve God?" This is the question no reader of this biblical book can avoid. Nor can we avoid attempting an answer. And when we define that faith, we successfully create greater boundaries within which we define our relationship with God and with others. Confirming the faith that we have softens and enriches the impact of any crisis that might come our way.

Importantly, most people have the experience of reckoning with aspects of their faith in God, with or without a crisis. But changes can occur in our faith, especially during times of crisis. Doubts about God can creep in. They did in Job. One either moves toward greater faith or suffers a diminished faith—both are defined by some level of wrestling with God. It's the quality and/or the quantity of communication that makes a significant difference. As Glatzer states, "The creation itself already means communication between Creator and creature. The just Creator gives to all his creatures his boundary, so that each may become fully itself."[8]

The Book of Job offers the perfect paradigm for reflecting on both our religious and spiritual needs now. It offers biblical, spiritual, and experiential treasure through Job's multifaceted questions and his personal life reflections. We are not always successful in wrestling with God as we attempt to work through some of our circumstances, especially those of seeming diabolical design.

The Book of Job lays down a well-paved road to a mature and deeply personal faith that is far beyond mere religiosity. It takes Job forty-two chapters to get there. With much debate, lots of recrimination, and unparalleled communion with and questioning of God, such faith emerges for Job through every human capacity: physical, emotional, psychological, and spiritual. Such faith grows out of the very painful human experiences of disease, loss of family, loss of wealth, broken relationships, and even estrangement from God. It's a faith that supersedes mere religious duty, tradition, or a sense of obligation. In both biblical Hebrew and Greek, the word *faith* is a verb, not a noun, although many Christians intuit it as something they have instead of something they do. Faith is behavior, not mere mental assent. In crises, we do not generally ask, "What do I believe?" Rather, we ask, "What do I do now *that* I believe?" This awareness should challenge us in presenting the faith to believers because the result renders them either victims or victors.

Four rounds of earthly dialogue between Job and his friends follow the dialogue in heaven between God and Satan, which reveals progressively intensifying levels of crisis for Job. However, any reader might gain significant spiritual renewal and a new boldness of faith that further enriches his or her relationship with God. Asking questions is not only indicative of one's inquisitive nature but also tantamount to one's will to live, survive, thrive, and achieve. So, think it neither strange nor obsessive that Job asks so many questions. May Job's questions drive us toward the wisdom and greater freedom of asking pertinent questions as we wrestle with self, others, life, and God. Consider:

- Is a life of faith just a series of glimpses into the eternal, or is our religious experience intended and expected to be far more than that?
- Where are the parameters of thought about God in our lives?
- Where are the boundaries of human-divine encounters, and how does Satan fit into that experience?

Human anguish pushes Job well beyond his preconceived boundaries and can also push us. Physical pain, mental distress, and spiritual anguish push Job to nearly curse God. He went far beyond just wanting to die or wishing he had never been born to actually cursing the moment he was conceived, which is a decision above any human pay grade. Before we can realize a more mature faith, we must be able to conceptualize the faithfulness of God within which we discover our moorings and rest in the faith needed to activate and navigate our lives. Such faith not only knows a powerful and benevolent transcendent being but is also capable of experiencing the immanence of God as sustainer and preserver of life.

The Latin phrase *Deus absconditus* ("hidden God") is rooted in religion and suggests that God should remain clothed in mystery. The Hebrew word *mistattêr* means "to hide oneself." Whether the idea that God is "hidden" is rooted in reverence or ignorance, we might understand this as putting God beyond our human grasp and understanding. But the Book of Job demonstrates that God desires to fully engage with us as God's creation spiritually, intellectually, emotionally, and especially within the depths of our existential angst.

In the end, Job declares that he had previously "heard of God," but finally, he testifies that he now sees God with his own eyes (42:5). He lobs his questions at God and leads us through his quizzical jungle of vain religion—initially insufficient to usher him into a rare, mature, and exceptional faith in God. When reached, such faith is like a golden thread woven into the tapestry of life, offering its beauty and power and highlighting life's meaning and purpose. Job inspires us with the evidence that faith in this God is not achieved without an inquiring mind, moral clarification, and spiritual agony.

Yale Professor Marvin Pope asserts that "Job's journey from despair to faith is the only way each mortal must go."[9] Mature faith is not synonymous with one's longevity as a church member, frequency of church attendance, nor breadth of church involvement. Job simply needs God to appear—*to just show up*—to shift him beyond all that he later declares he had only "been hearing about God" before he could finally "see God" for himself. That encounter ushers in not only the deepest sense of awe while diminishing his doubts but also brings him to a level of introspection that leads Job to a sense of self-contempt in God's presence.

In the throes of a crisis, believers might be pushed to question themselves, their past, their family and friends, as well as God. Like Job, an honest reappraisal of self and of *self-in-situation* just might be the necessary route to take. The Book of Job helps move personal faith from spiritual dormancy to a level of vibrancy impossible without self-examination. Job grew because Job wrestled. Seen as wise, wealthy, and worthy, Job is not viewed as sinless but as righteous in God's assessment because he faithfully performs covenantal behaviors such as sacrifices for himself and his family to cover their sins.

The Book of Job provides a glimpse of the vacuous area between our development as humans and the driving forces that help to develop our faith. Though on parallel tracks, human growth and spiritual maturing are not equal in substance nor rate of speed. The church has taught the content of faith but has regrettably too often stopped short of differentiating faith from mere belief, church attendance, or religious activity.

The spiritual vitality we gain from studying this biblical book is nothing short of amazing. It deepens our intimate knowledge of God, creating a richer relationship while fortifying us as believers to meet the challenges and crises of life that might befall us. We begin our deep study of Job in chapter 1, where we become privy to a debate between God and Satan, framed as legal proceedings. Chapter 2 offers a new perspective on Job's wife, who has been maligned by commentators and readers alike for millennia. Consequently, chapter 3 will help transform the "Why me?" syndrome into a different perspective that just might make life more positive and pleasant. In chapter 4, we will look closer at Job's friends, who initially come to comfort but inflict harm instead. Chapter 5 reflects on how wisdom shapes faith, and chapter 6 examines how questions deepen our faith. In chapter 7, we see how to grow from asking "Why me?" about our problems to a "Why not me?" point of view. In chapter 8, we learn how God works through our questions. In chapter 9, we witness the completion of Job's faith transformation, and in chapter 10, we rejoice as his life begins anew. Finally, in chapter 11, I offer reflections on the role of lament in Job's life and how it may spur and energize the church today.

Crises of a profound nature have shaped my life but never beyond the assurance of God's presence to see me through them. Therefore, I can bring to this literary endeavor a high Christological orientation and concern for humanity's personal well-being and soteriological needs as we find ourselves in numerous crises. Like the Shona people in Southern Africa, I see God as "the one who can turn things upside down," suggesting God's immutability—changing things while yet remaining unchangeable. Come with me into one of the most spectacular divine-human encounters ever recorded in literature!

Notes

1. Samuel G. Candler, "Why Is the Book of Job Even in the Bible?" October 22, 2018, https://www.cathedralatl.org/goodfaithpostings/why-is-the-book-of-job-even-in-the-bible/#:.
2. Tokunboh Adeyemo, ed., *Africa Bible Commentary* (Grand Rapids: Zondervan, 2006), 572.
3. *Ancient Christian Commentary on Scripture*, ed. Thomas C. Oden (Downers Grove, IL: InterVarsity, 2006), XIX.
4. E. Glenn Hinson, *Seekers after Mature Faith: Deepening Devotional Life with Help from Christians of Past and Present* (Nashville: Broadman, 1968), 46.
5. Hinson, 572.
6. Nahum N. Glatzer, *The Dimensions of Job* (New York: Schocken, 1969), 185.
7. Jeff A. Benner, "Good," Ancient Hebrew Research Center, accessed June 2, 2023, https://www.ancient-hebrew.org/definition/good.htm.
8. Glatzer, *Dimensions of Job*, 63.
9. Marvin H. Pope, *The Anchor Bible: A New Translation* (Garden City, NY: Doubleday, 1985), LXXXIII.

Chapter One

THE COURT IS IN SESSION (Job 1)

Establishing the Case (Job 1:1-12)

Psalm 103:19 declares: "The LORD has established his throne in heaven, and his kingdom rules overall." That's where we find ourselves as the biblical saga of Job opens! Welcome to a courtroom that is well beyond supreme. It's sovereign. And God is on the bench as Judge and has already pronounced this human named Job innocent. Not only is Job pronounced innocent, but God uses the religious terminology "blameless and upright" (Job 1:8). God has known Job since before Job was conceived, making it clear that Job belongs to God. And God is not about to give up that ownership nor authority over Job's life. Being sovereign, God has no need, nor might we require God to recuse himself, having known Job from embryo to earthling. Under God's judicial prudence, Job is put under special protection that originates in the courtroom of heaven. God's own celestial courtroom is conducted with an assemblage of angels within the boundaries of creation and in God's own sovereign kingdom.

But a non-angel who is none other than every human earthling's accuser appears in their midst. In Hebrew, he is called "the Satan" (haś·śā·ṭān, הַשָּׂטָן), which is translated as accuser and understood as the adversary of God. But the Gospels just have "Satan." Satan is in this divine courtroom to prosecute his own trumped-up case against Job. He attempts to prove that the sovereign God cannot hold on to those who are in covenant with him. In his prosecutorial effort, Satan seeks to break the bonds of God's well-established covenant, which Job's behavior confirms that he takes quite seriously. Job offers sacrifices to God not just for his own sins but also for the sins his children may have committed. God's protective care of Job enrages Satan, prompting him to taunt God to just "stretch out your hand and strike everything he has" (verse 11).

Satan Presents His Case

Perhaps the most important question raised—since it drives the sequences of the book—is the question Satan asks: "'Does Job fear God for nothing?' . . . 'Have you not put a hedge around him and his household and everything he has? You have blessed the work of his hands, so that his flocks and herds are spread throughout the land. But now stretch out your hand and strike everything he has, and he will surely curse you to your face'" (1:9-11).

Satan views this divine-human relationship as quite superficial and transactional in nature. Satan believes that Job is only faithful to God because of the wealth he has acquired. Consequently, he suggests Job's need to appease God is derived from the fear of losing what he has and being afraid that the well of his blessings could dry up. Job expresses profound anguish but never any sense of being afraid of the God he daily seeks to serve.

As with Job, our adversary Satan intentionally misreads not only our intentions but our motives as well. Yet God is not deceived by Satan's antics. Though accused of being afraid of God, Job shows his reverence for God by offering daily sacrifices in response to the covenantal relationship he has experienced with God. The sacrifices are evidence of Job's faithfulness to what he perceives as a binding agreement with God; he is true to the one he considers the source of his wealth and well-being. Fear does not define Job's relationship with the sovereign God. Rather, his reverence spawns a sense of obedience and adoration. That's what Satan seeks to distort while also suggesting in the courtroom that God has Job in protective custody from Satan's adversarial plot and thus cannot be touched without the removal of God's protective powers. Satan asks how he could even test Job while God has placed such a protective hedge around him and all that is his.

In his role as prosecutor, Satan accuses Job of serving God only on a transactional basis: Because *you bless me, I'll serve you; I'll worship you because I don't want to lose my wealth.* However, there is no basis in fact. Satan simply acts out the role of the accuser: to accuse. Satan asserts that what really motivates Job to serve God is that Job has been and wants continually to be blessed with wealth, prestige, family, workers, and animals. Satan also asserts that there are no other grounds for Job to serve God. He offers "Exhibit A" to the Sovereign court when he declares that if God would stretch out his hand against Job, then Job would curse God to his face.

Gustavo Gutierrez, professor of theology at the Catholic University in Lima, Peru, says that "it is impossible for Satan to deny that Job is a good and devout man. What he questions is rather the disinterestedness of Job's service to God, his lack of concern for a reward. Satan objects not to Job's works but to their motivation: Job's behavior, [Satan] says, is not for nothing."[1] God temporarily suspends his own authority over Job's possessions, living, and activities, but not over Job's life, by declaring to Satan, "Very well, then, everything he has is in your power, but on the man himself do not lay a finger" (1:12). With this, Satan departs the heavenly courtroom. He is determined to prove his case as a prosecutor.

Importantly, Satan had to leave God's presence to do the evil he had planned in his Exhibit A against Job.

Though it may occasionally seem so, God never gives full rein over our lives to the adversary. The ultimate power of God is the capacity to sustain his sovereignty; in that, we can put the weight of our faith, which no adversary can ever destroy. I could easily list a hundred traumatic moments I've experienced since I was four and a half years old. But at no time did I ever think of exiting the covenant I enjoy with God. I have always enjoyed at least a scintilla of faith—a residual amount that my dilemma could not sap. Job's losses took him to the edge of the worst abyss we might imagine, but the covenant held. Having outlived my immediate family, no other earthly possessions mattered. My mother passed suddenly in 1982, my sister passed suddenly in 2000, and my dad passed suddenly in 2012. The consequent aloneness was profound. Somehow, God confirmed for me that the umbilical cord of faith was unsevered, and my capacity to live by the strength of that covenant and by that faith might have been weakened but not depleted.

The Trials of Life (Job 1:13-22)

In rapid succession, storms, thieves, and murderers bedevil Job's life, filling it with unquestionable sorrow, grief, and anger within unimaginable short spans of time. Ravaging storms sweep away Job's sons and daughters. Marauders steal his oxen and donkeys and kill his servants. Fire sweeps down and kills sheep and shepherds. Raiding parties make off with Job's camels and kill the last of Job's surviving servants. Profound losses comprise Satan's Exhibit A, which fails to produce the curse he predicts will spew from Job's mouth. Despite these hardships and losses, Job never utters any curse words toward God! But Satan isn't done tormenting Job yet. Aware of his failure, Satan asks for one more chance and then presents Exhibit B. God, the sovereign Judge, extends some judicial latitude, knowing that Satan failed in his initial attempt to make Job curse God in anger, grief, or despair.

In round two, Job's bodily disease and physical discomfort eclipse the painful losses of family and treasures he has suffered. Imagine such losses in your life or such havoc robbing you of your well-being, happiness, stability, sense of control, or power in your own life. Satan is happy in his new sense of power as the adversary but unaware that his goal to destroy the relationship that is intact between God and Job is not possible. Job is miserable, but God's sovereignty remains.

God knows the limitations of our strengths and the power of our endurance. Remember that Satan did not take Job from God. No, God offered or surrendered Job to the adversary: "Have you considered my servant Job?" (1:8; 2:3).

I could preach a million sermons on that one question. Having listened to many lawyers discuss legal strategies, one I vividly recall is, "Never ask a question to which you don't already know the answer." That strategy may well have been gleaned from the Book of Job as God presided over his courtroom. Though God had kept faithful watch over Job, Satan had spied out Job's reverent behavior toward God and his intact relationship. God knew that Satan knew every aspect of Job's life. But with all that Satan thought he knew, he had no power to afflict Job's life or body beyond repair.

In trying times, where does that leave those of us whose faith might be in tatters or whose hope seems to have slipped from its foundation or whose life has lost its moorings? These initial chapters of Job can help to rebuild our faith once we realize that although we are under fire from Satan, we remain unmistakably in the powerful hands of God—a bond that any adversary might seek to undermine but never break. Having entered into a covenant with God, we cannot keep ourselves; even our worst adversary has to admit that God never withdraws his sovereign protection from our lives.

Covenants Set Parameters

I find it spiritually curious that twice God asks Satan, "Have you considered my servant Job?" (1:8; 2:3) and not vice versa. To me, this divine inquiry suggests a previous or ongoing conversation between God and the adversary. I ask, is Satan out to prove something, or is God? Perhaps both cases are true. Satan is perennially seeking ways to dismantle what God creates. In contrast, God uses Satan's unsuccessful attempts as great evidence that the center of his creation is holding fast, that is, that God's relationship with his covenant people is not being undermined nor canceled, nor will God allow it to be destroyed. God is about to prove to Satan that no power can break the bond God has with creation, nor can Satan dismantle that relationship. God sets the boundary of creation with humanity through covenants that Satan has no power to cancel.

To fully comprehend the Book of Job, we must perceive the context in which this divine-human connection occurs. Clearly, Job is in a covenant relationship with God. This is first signaled by God declaring some measure of righteousness—*right living* or functioning—that is present in Job's life. Job meets God's expectations of behavior within the bond of their covenantal relationship. God never declares Job sinless—God simply declares Job *blameless and upright* (1:8; 2:3), meaning that Job's pattern of behavior in religious acts meets God's requirements. What's more, Job's life reflects those qualities through the offerings he makes for the sins of his children as well as the offerings he makes for his own sins. Job's choosing to sit on an ash heap is another suggestive detail inferring religious boundaries defining his life and living. The ash heap symbolizes deep sorrow but an even deeper sense of repentance. Ashes are what our bodies return to after death, but in life, ashes reflect one's profound sorrow and dismay—a sifting or profound examination of life. Job is at the lowest point, having had everything taken from him—family and farm, wealth and health, power, and physical ability. Everything is gone except his wife.

When we understand the quality of Job's relationship with God, we can subsequently fathom why Satan, knowing of Job's faithfulness to God, finds it desirable to try to ruin Job. Job sees all he possesses as evidence of God's blessings in his life: children, livestock, workers, land, status in the community, great health, and a wife. But Satan's question is, "Can Job be faithful to such covenanted expectations if he isn't going to be so abundantly blessed?" Satan challenges God by mischaracterizing the reasons God's servants serve God. Even Satan knows that serving God is not an easy task. Will Job still serve God if he experiences not just a slight reversal of such blessings but the loss of everything up to the very brink of his life?

So, God decides to let the test roll on, permitting Satan to strip Job of every blessing and his good fortune. But God restricts Satan from taking Job's life. Satan now has Job in his crosshairs. Job is not out of God's sight, nor is he eliminated from God's plans. As believers, we are often unaware that Satan endeavors to "de-create" any aspect of God's creation by seeking to usurp God's power and even to undermine God's faithfulness or God's ability to be trusted. This raises the question of theodicy, which has troubled theologians and believers for millennia.

Theodicy

How would you respond if someone asked you, "Who created evil?" Your faith tells you that God created the universe with you in it then pronounced, "It is good." So, from where did evil emerge? We all know the biblical account of sin in the Garden of Eden, but Job had committed no sin. So, how do we square this circle? It's a debate and dilemma that remains unclear for many. With evil all around us, how do we vindicate divine goodness and providence in the face of it? This remains the task of theodicy. It's formed by the Greek word θεός (*theós*), meaning "god" and δίκη (*díkē*), meaning justice, which is usually translated as "justifying God." The word was birthed by the seventeenth-century German mathematician, philosopher, scientist, and diplomat Gottfried Wilhelm von Leibniz. And for all those specialties, he was called a polymath. Theodicy wrestles with the question of why a good God permits the manifestation of evil in the lives of the humans he created and loves.

For many religious folks, it is too challenging a subject to tackle. But Leibniz raised the mundane to sublime levels when he used a mere doughnut—yes, a doughnut—to define evil within the broader conceptual space of theodicy. It is the most striking description or explanation of such a complex subject I have discovered. He claimed that evil has no positive reality but is a mere privation or lack of being—nothingness or emptiness, as it were. As I understand his thought, evil takes away or deprives us of something. In other words, sin deprives us of the good that God pronounced over all of creation. And for Job, the list was quite long.

Leibniz declared that evil has no more (separate) reality than the hole in the center of a doughnut. Making a doughnut does not require combining two components: the cake and the hole. The cake is all there is to the doughnut, and the hole is just the "privation of cake." It, therefore, would be silly to say that making the doughnut requires both the cake and the hole to exist. The hole is the by-product of causing a particular kind of cake to exist. Thus, we need not assume any additional cause for the hole beyond that assumed for the creation of the cake. Whether belief in an all-good, omnipotent God is compatible with the existence of evil in this world is a question of great importance in many people's lives, which leads some to believe in God and others to lose their faith.

In other words, the upshot of Leibniz's pastry metaphor is this: given that evil, like the hole, is merely privation, it necessitates no separate cause. His conclusion was that God does not causally contribute to evil because evil per se is not a (separate) thing and, therefore, requires no cause to exist. He saw evil as misery, hardship, and poverty, all of which are lack or deprivation or the uncreated part of a doughnut. He is saying that God did not and does not create evil; rather, evil is the experience of privation in the world of abundance that God has created.[2]

Both good and evil are clearly manifested in our world and penetrate our lives. However, the quality of our relationship with God depends greatly on our depth of knowledge and awareness about both good and evil so that we can best navigate our way through life as people of faith. We mere humans wrestle with evil in light of the existence of God, as did Job. We seek to vindicate God's divine attributes, especially God's holiness and justice, while not denying the existence of moral and physical evil.

Anglican lay theologian and author C. S. Lewis believed, relative to theodicy, that three realities exist from which we cannot escape, nor can we dispute biblically within the context of our lived experience.

> Yes, God is completely good.
> Yes, God is completely powerful.
> Yes, pain and suffering exists.[3]

The existence of pain does not negate the presence of an omnipotent, loving God. When understood in the fullness of its context, we realize that God's very presence provides meaning and hope even amid the pain. The theological concept of theodicy tries to reconcile these three realities in an attempt to understand why God is thought to allow evil in the world to plague the people he created and loves.

The Hebrew patriarch Abraham asked, "Shall not the Judge of all the earth do what is just?" (Genesis 18:25, NRSV), affirming his belief in a just God. From the Christian faith,

Jesus offered an agrarian analysis of the presence of good and evil in our lives. He included a timeline by sharing that God would allow the wheat (good) and tares (evil) to grow up together, and at some ultimate point in time, God would separate them (Matthew 13:24-30). So, neither good nor evil is outside the realm of God's capacity to govern or manage his creation.

Everything that is of any value in our lives has been tested, from drinks to cars, makeup to mattresses, medical products to math equations, and roads to relationships. So why shouldn't our faith be tested—not for God's benefit but to enrich our personal faith journey? Our awareness of evil (various misfortunes in our lives) is not intended to destroy us but to nurture and develop mature faith. God does not need to put us through such paces or such experiences to unveil for himself the strength of our relationship. Rather, such experiences reveal God to us ever more deeply. Having chosen to grant humans free will, God needs believers to know whether their devotion is genuine. God's search for our commitment underlies the harrowing tests of Moses and Abraham, whom God commands to sacrifice his son Isaac (Genesis 22). However, many feel that, in the end, theodicy fails to offer a convincing, rational explanation for evil.[4]

Despite Job's excruciating moral, spiritual, and physical pain, he is not delivered of his humanity. Whether Job, you, or me, our humanity ensures us great freedom, limited only by proscribed boundaries of our knowledge and power. We humans experience within ourselves a microcosm of God's power over good and evil. But does not any evil that strikes our lives initially leave us feeling powerless? Do we not usually need to regroup from its onslaught before we can muster the power to address whatever horror, brokenness, mishap, devastation, or deprivation we have experienced?

Stephen J. Vicchio, noted author and theologian, concludes that "God at long last replies" (with speeches of his own) to Job's query in speeches that have been characterized as "one spectacular irrelevance to the plot of the book."[5] Vicchio describes the speeches in which God gives Job a new sense of himself and a grander sense of their relationship as "an overwhelming and stunning rhetorical blast in which God depicts the divine creative power and glory in such a way that Job's rebellion ceases. Overwhelmed by God's creative power and glory, Job comes to see his own suffering in a new light."[6]

Let us be clear at the outset what exactly is at stake. The Greek philosopher Epicurus gave us an early formulation of the problem of evil and a logical problem that deals with believing in God:

> God either wishes to take away evils and is unable; or he is able and unwilling; or he is neither willing nor able; or he is both willing and able. If he is willing and unable, he is feeble, which is not in accordance with the character of God; if he is able and unwilling, he is envious, which is equally at variance with God; if he is neither willing nor able, he is both feeble and envious, and therefore not God; if he is both willing and able, which alone is suitable for God, from what source then are evils? Or why does he not remove them?[7]

As in Job's story, is it not Satan who similarly attempts to turn our blessings into curses within the scope of our lives? Satan believes we should be deprived of our blessings, attempting to drive a wedge between us and God. As our adversary, he labors to weaken the bond God fashioned with us subsequent to creation via a covenant relationship. After piling loss upon loss upon loss, Satan now strikes a near-death blow to Job's body. However, Satan's goal is to steal what Job yet possesses in his heart and soul: the very reason he serves God!

Questions for Reflection or Response

1. What has God uniquely created in you that Satan has sought to "de-create" or deprive from your life?
2. Reading the first chapter of Job, has your perception of Satan changed? How?
3. I now see evil more as what I'm deprived of than as a separate causal force. And you—how do you define evil in the context of your life?

Notes

1. Gustavo Gutierrez, *On Job: God-Talk and the Suffering of the Innocent* (Maryknoll, NY: Orbis Books, 1987), 4.
2. Michael J. Murray and Sean Greenberg, "Leibniz on the Problem of Evil," *Stanford Encyclopedia of Philosophy Archive*, ed. Edward N. Zalta (Winter 2016), first published January 4, 1998, revised February 27, 2013, https://plato.stanford.edu/archives/win2016/entries/leibniz-evil/.
3. Jana Harmon, "C. S. Lewis on the Problem of Pain," *Knowing and Doing*, September 1, 2012, C. S. Lewis Institute, https://www.cslewisinstitute.org/resources/c-s-lewis-on-the-problem-of-pain/.
4. James Crenshaw, "Theodicy in the Hebrew Bible," September 8, 2021, https://www.bibleodyssey.org:443/en/people/related-articles/theodicy-in-the-hebrew-bible.
5. Stephen J. Vicchio, *The Voice from the Whirlwind: The Problem of Evil and the Modern World* (Eugene, OR: Wipf & Stock, 2006), 177.
6. Vicchio, 178.
7. John Holroyd, "The Good, the Bad, and Theodicy," Philosophy Now, 2019, accessed June 2, 2023, https://philosophynow.org/issues/133/The_Good_The_Bad_and_Theodicy. John Holroyd taught philosophy and religion for many years.

Chapter Two

TRIAL OF A DIFFERENT SORT (Job 2)

From the Courtroom to the Ash Heap

Initially, Job's trial was in the courtroom of the sovereign God with Job's adversary serving as prosecutor against him. Now he experiences a trial of a different sort: the ash heap. Interestingly, the final Old Testament reference to Satan is in this prologue to Job.[1] Job's adversaries are three men who come to visit him as friends. However, they only have the power to afflict him with their words. Job is already sitting on his mound of profound sorrow in a state of repentance, yet his three friends rip the scabs off his sores, so to speak, with their onslaught of accusations. Their vain religious rhetoric neither honors God (as God declares at the end) nor themselves, much less the one they have come to console.

Job sits on the ash heap in anguish of soul, with no end to his suffering in sight. An ash heap in the Eastern world was a pile of ashes left after garbage had been burned. It was a very unusual place of seeming uselessness for humans that portrayed some sense of repentance albeit with Job virtually swearing he had done nothing deserving of such discomfort. It wasn't a private space; rather, this public arena was open for anyone to see. Job's "friends," whose eyes were open but whose hearts were closed to Job, came with virtually no level of compassion except for their seven days of silence. And those 168 hours of silence seemed to have served only to buttress the onslaught of condemnation these "friends" were soon to unleash on Job!

Job's Wife

Job sits silent for seven long days while his three friends and his wife look on helplessly. Mrs. Job is often not portrayed as a sympathetic or compassionate character by those who study Job in this dramatic biblical saga rife with pain and destruction. When we show her no sympathy, we, along with preachers and commentators, neglect the reality that Job's losses of children, workers, cattle, and wealth were also her losses. Those were *her* children. All ten of their children were seemingly past the age of twelve, which is the covenant age of accountability. Those were *her* farmworkers whom, as the lady of the house, she ensured were fed and their families cared for while they worked for her husband. She was fully invested in all they had built. Yet she is said to have uttered those infamous words that assured her a peculiar place in biblical, human, and church history: "Are you still maintaining your integrity? Curse God and die!" (Job 2:9).

Curiously, within the first three chapters of Job, six different words translated as *curse* are used, none of which are the Hebrew words spoken by Job's wife:

> "Opened Job his mouth, and cursed his day" (3:1, KJV).
> וַיְקַלֵּל
> "Let them curse it that curse the day" (3:8, KJV).
> יִקְּבֻהוּ אֹרְרֵי־יוֹם
> "Let them curse it that curse the day" (3:8, KJV). יִקְּבֻהוּ
> "Have sinned, and cursed God" (1:5, KJV). וּבֵרֲכוּ

> "And touch all that he hath, and he will curse thee to thy face" (1:11, KJV). יְבָרְכֶךָּ:
> "And he will curse thee to thy face (2:5, KJV). יְבָרְכֶךָּ:

I have heard more sermons preached about Job's wife's words than about any other part of this biblical book. In contrast to Job's struggle not to allow his losses and disease to provoke him to curse God, her few words are heavily weighted as a reproach to her husband. Some preachers misrepresent her words or intentions toward her husband. As Job tends to his servants, farm, and animals, Mrs. Job evidently takes great joy in nurturing a family who loved being together in celebration of one another's lives. A man of such high esteem as Job would also have a wife held in great esteem by the community. With him being "the richest man," she likely lived a queenly lifestyle. No doubt she was united with Job in grieving. She reacts to his distorted appearance and his agonizing pain as well as sharing in the loss of their ten children. Is it all just a bit too much for her to face? Can we spare at least one tear for her as well?

Along with Job, his wife is also stripped of everything that brought meaning and prosperity to their lives. Could she perhaps be at the point of giving up a bit sooner than him? Still today her few words inflame any conversational or sermonic reference to her. They mar any thought of her experiencing extreme anguish or compassion for her husband. Job, while in unspeakable pain, does not condemn her; rather, in this moment, he simply compares her usually wise ways to those of foolish women: "You speak as one of the foolish women would speak" (2:10, ESV).

To Job, his wife just did not sound like herself. As author and pastor James Thornton says, "Sudden loss has a way of clouding our judgment, distorting our view of reality and of God."[2] Significantly, nowhere in this book does God rebuke her. Nor does God name any other woman as Job's wife or as the mother of his second set of ten children. In the end, God declares that Job's friends are wrong, but God never condemns Mrs. Job. Instead, God blesses her with a new set of children, which biblically magnifies how pleased God was with her as Job's wife. That is an amazing reality that has been lost on some for a few millennia.

The word that she supposedly uses to castigate her husband is arguably mistranslated throughout all these years. When the Hebrew word *bārak̲* is used in this form in the Hebrew Bible, it is usually translated as "bless"—except when it falls from the lips of Job's wife.

> Numbers 23:25: "Neither . . . bless them at all!"
> Deuteronomy 33:11: "Bless all his skills, O Lord."
> 1 Chronicles 4:10: "Oh, that you would bless me."
> Psalm 132:15: "I will bless her with abundant provisions."

Hebrew people within their covenant relationship with God would never utter the words "curse God" to anyone since that would be tantamount to cursing God themselves. Given the circumstances in which it is uttered, it has a special possible nuance. For example, if this word is uttered in the temple, it signals encouragement to praise God. Conversely, if the same word is uttered in a negative life situation, it is suggestive of making one's peace with God before moving through the portals of death. Realistically, is that not what Job's wife was anticipating for her husband given his repulsive health condition? With knowledge of or sensitivity to this nuanced difference, preachers still castigate Job's wife, women throughout subsequent millennia, and even women today because of this incorrect rendering of that one word placed in her mouth. The *Jewish Women's Archive* refers to her as "a victim of divine affliction."[3]

Mrs. Job is mentioned indirectly only once more in the book. Job declares that he would trade her off with other men *if* he had sinned with other women, which he hadn't (see 31:9–10). Even Augustine is said to have labeled her "the devil's accomplice,"[4] and French theologian and ecclesiastical statesman John Calvin reportedly called her "a diabolical fury."[5] But the Hebrew language does not bear that out. Their words seem overblown to me, even libelous, because what is clearly understandable is not necessarily accepted.

The close of the book confirms that Job's wife remains faithful to the God they worshipped, the God who once again not only filled their coffers and their lives but also filled her womb with blessings that the world admired. Sadly, she can only watch the agony her husband experiences, while his seemingly unending list of questions echoes in her ears and tears at her heart:

> Why is light given to those in misery,
> and life to the bitter of soul,
> to those who long for death that does not come,
> who search for it more than for hidden treasure,
> who are filled with gladness
> and rejoice when they reach the grave?
> Why is life given to a man
> whose way is hidden,
> whom God has hedged in?
> For sighing has become my daily food;
> my groans pour out like water.
> What I feared has come upon me;
> what I dreaded has happened to me.
> I have no peace, no quietness;
> I have no rest, but only turmoil.
>
> —3:20-26

Few women in history have borne the magnitude of misogynistic scorn that Mrs. Job has. Perhaps even fewer have had their words so misinterpreted as she. And let me go a bit further: even fewer females have been so rhetorically bludgeoned with the "weapon" of biblical writ. Those who have assaulted her brief mention in our canon need to repent for such a mischaracterization because Scripture is beyond contradiction that God was in her corner—blessing her, not condemning her in the least. On that I will do my happy dance!

In my years of church life, I have heard ten times more sermons about Job's wife than I have heard about Job. That one reality, though very harsh, is profound in and of itself since it reveals a degree of animus against her that the rest of us females have had to endure over those same millennia. Sadly, many women in the pews have cheered on the sermonic assault even though they would never mouth such words to their own husbands. From Eve to Ruth to Mary to Luke's "certain women" to Priscilla—*and many more*—women have filled glorious roles both in God's creation and biblical history. It is in the annals of church history that women have too often been sadly and sorely diminished purportedly on biblical grounds! From now on, let us speak the truth about Mrs. Job and honor her in our churches with a sermon or two that corrects this previous biblical translation of the word "bless" and centuries of misinterpretation. That could be a true celebration as we overcome our previous ignorance of the Word of God. As the saying goes, "When you know better, you do better." God is waiting.

Job did respond to his wife with a comparison to "foolish women," but that is possibly the crux of the initial mistranslation. Some still put the negative intent on Mrs. Job when it should have been on her husband all the time. Perhaps he thought (given that his body was covered in painful, pus-filled sores), *Woman, you want me to bless God now? In this condition? Sitting on this ash heap? With no end in sight? Well, I am never going to curse God, but neither am I ready to bless God just yet.* Let us allow Job to bear his own responsibility for what was potentially his moment of wallowing in his momentary affliction.

And the worst is yet to come, as Job enters moral and spiritual combat with his friends who have come to sit with him and mourn with him yet castigate him after hearing of his plight. They feign compassion while sitting with him for seven days and nights. Silence is their respectful preamble to the verbal sparring that is about to begin concerning the substance of Job's religious life—his faith or the lack thereof. Before examining Job's time of suffering in silence, I invite you to pause and reflect on the following questions.

Questions for Reflection or Response

1. How did you respond when you first heard or read about Mrs. Job?
2. What is your impression of Mrs. Job now?
3. In similar dire straits, what might your love for your mate compel you to say?
4. How might you address this matter in your own church Bible study?
5. How open to this transforming reality about Mrs. Job might women in your church be?

Notes

1. Paige Lanier Chargois, "Faith Development: The Job Paradigm, a Pastoral Model" (DMin diss., United Theological Seminary, 1994), 71.
2. James L. Thornton, "The Most Misunderstood Woman in the Bible: Why Job's Wife May Have Gotten a Bad Rap," Everyone's Apostolic, accessed June 3, 2023, https://everyonesapostolic.com/?s=The+Most+Misunderstood+Woman.
3. Ilana Pardes, "Wife of Job: Bible," The Shalvi/Hyman Encyclopedia of Jewish Women, December 31, 1999, Jewish Women's Archive, https://jwa.org/encyclopedia/article/wife-of-job-bible.
4. Philip Schaff, trans., Augustine of Hippo, On the Creed: A Sermon to the Catechumens: On the Holy Trinity, Doctrinal Treatises, Moral Treatises, vol. 3, A Select Library of the Nicene and Post-Nicene Fathers of the Christian Church, First Series (Buffalo, NY: Christian Literature Company, 1887), 372.
5. Arthur Golding, et al., *Sermons of Master John Calvin Upon the Booke of Job*, Ninth Sermon on the Second Chapter of Job (Pennsylvania: Banner of Truth Trust, 2022), 40.

Chapter Three

"WHY ME?" SUFFERING IN SILENCE (Job 3)

As the Book of Job focuses on the suffering, silence, and triumph of one man, Stephen J. Vicchio refers to it as a "supreme literary masterpiece—one of the greatest creations of world literature."[1] Such a laudable comment tremendously heightens the book's biblical value to us as well, regardless of whether we perchance find ourselves in similar straits. The Book of Job takes us to the depths of the most valued human relationships—spouse, family, friends—and with God. Though poetically written, as one of the Bible's five wisdom books, its insights and wisdom have nourished the minds and souls of folks across the human spectrum for millennia. Reading Job can be deeply impactful for any serious reader as the book is a touchstone for our times. We struggle with racial unrest and with deep political divisions—both of which involve "othering"[2] on a scale beyond our recent experiences. Churches have divided over social differences and even over public health responses in recent times. A multiyear pandemic has left in its wake many people who are isolated, suffering alone, and wondering what tomorrow will bring. Being tested and tried, some people, like Job, wonder and stifle the scream, "Why me?"

Within the proverbial horrors and afflictions we experience, we also search for practical answers, wisdom from on high, and insights from antiquity. In such traumatic moments, we are often without explanations and, in frustration, can even be a horror to ourselves, recoiling into the recesses of our humanity until some sense is made of that trauma or misfortune. We, too, might utter a natural query of "What just happened?" or "Why me?" Either could be a natural response. Job is no exception. As Rabbi Harold Kushner writes,

> Human beings are meaning-makers . . . and the concept of fairness is uniquely human. The Bible describes God [as] creating an orderly world, a world in which everything has its place. . . . Only with the creation of the first human beings does the orderliness of the world give way to the possibility of unpredictability. . . . And only then does the question of the world's fairness, its moral as well as its physical reliability, emerge.[3]

We raise issues of fairness or justice too. Our sense of deservedness may spawn rage well beyond our usual inquisitiveness. We are not satisfied until we draw some meaning out of our dilemma into our lives.

In times such as these today, we find ourselves asking questions about God and the meaning of life. Questions are essential to learning and growing. Many fields use questions as the starting point for diagnosing, gaining new skills, and more. It is natural to ask questions and adjust our thinking as we receive responses (or nonresponses). Questions have been significant in my professional career as a journalist, given that the quality of an interviewer's questions determines the quality of responses. The questions who, what, when, where, and why are primary interrogatives that journalists ask to ferret out the essentials of the story at hand. By asking more than a hundred questions (depending on which translation one uses), Job can be viewed as the interviewer and God as the interviewee. The following are a sampling of Job's questions as Job wrestled with God:

> "Why is life given to a man whose way is hidden, whom God has hedged in?" (3:23).
> "What strength do I have, that I should still hope? What prospects, that I should be patient?" (6:11).
> "Why do you not pardon my offenses and forgive my sins?" (7:21).
> "Who has resisted [God] and come out unscathed?" (9:4).
> "Give me, O God, the pledge you demand. Who else will put up security for me?" (17:3).
> "What would we gain by praying to [the Almighty]?" (21:15).
> "For what hope have the godless when they are cut off, when God takes away their life?" (27:8).
> "For what is our lot from God above, our heritage from the Almighty on high?" (31:2).

Job's questions are pertinent to his situation.

In general, we tend to think we must have ready answers, and over our lifetime, we are not usually taught that, instead, more questions are needed. We are socialized to think that to spew answers at any given moment is what best reflects one's intelligence; however, quite the opposite is true. We cannot know the answers until we know what the questions are. I heard of a church recently whose rector chose a novel approach for the church's way of planning their programs and events for the new year. In advance of their end-of-the-year planning session, she had them submit questions they felt they needed to raise. Then, based on those questions, the congregation came together to plan. Their questions had already moved them beyond the superficial thoughts about what ministries and programs to have in the new year, allowing them to offer more substantive ministries that they felt would strengthen their church, be meaningful to their community, and bring glory to God. Such a process seems quite novel for many congregations. Their questions became the seedbed out of which a beautiful "garden" of service beyond themselves could be accomplished; plus, with such buy-in from the very beginning, greater success was assured.

Job moves from questioning to despair. Though some of Job's questions are rhetorical, Job knows that his conversation is primarily with God and beyond his friends. The preponderance of questions in the Book of Job is one of the major things that attracted me to dig deeper into this book. A degree in psychology stirred me to lift him off the page and put him on the couch to care about the pain and obvious existential angst he is experiencing. Losing his children is one thing, but nearly as significant is his loss of status and stature in the community. Either of those elements can powerfully diminish the sense of meaning in our lives. One's loss of status can sometimes be more personally impactful than the loss of a family member. Although Job laments over the time when his children were still with him (29:12), he spends most of chapters 29 and 30 citing the quality of respect he enjoyed in his town only to, now, have his neighbors mock him.

Like Job, we cannot live without answers—even if it takes more than a hundred questions to pursue them. As meaning-makers, we, at times, desperately search for the wisdom to put the pieces of the puzzle of our lives together in some meaningful way. We not only deeply crave reason to resolve our problems, but the concept of fairness feels as if it is woven into our DNA. Rabbi Kushner added that some explanations of "human suffering leave us with an image of a mean, vindictive deity who may command our fear but who does not deserve our worship."[4] Such is not the case with Job, as we shall soon see.

To best understand the Book of Job, we need to understand the literary context within which it sits. After all, the Bible is not so much a singular book as it is a library of books.

While the Hebrew Bible contains history books and instruction manuals, it contains works of prophecy as well as poetry and narrative. In *Man Is Not Alone*, Rabbi Abraham Heschel declares that the Bible, containing many genres, is primarily not humanity's vision of God but God's vision of humanity. The Bible, he says, is God's anthropology, dealing with humanity and the nature of God. Job is on the journey of reconciling his beliefs about God and finding clarity in what others have told him about God that he has learned "through the hearing of the ear."[5]

Of the sixty-six books in the Bible, Job is one of only four, namely, Proverbs, Ecclesiastes, Job, and Song of Solomon, along with some psalms, classified as wisdom literature. Although it includes some poetry, it is not defined by that genre. Other parts of the Hebrew canon offer the Torah, or Jewish law, narratives of history, poetry, prophetic, and apocalyptic literature. It is Job, however, who asks, "But where can wisdom be found?" (28:12). Dr. Tokunboh Adeyemo helps to answer that question, "We can scan the earth, the sea and the heavens but cannot find wisdom. Nor can we buy it with all the gems we possess . . . The end of the human search for wisdom is intimated in the words 'God understands the way to it and he alone knows where it dwells' (Job 28:23). And then God articulates the essence of wisdom, 'and to shun evil is understanding.' (28:28). That is the message of the book, as incarnated in and exemplified by Job."[6] However, it is declared in 28:23 [that] only God understands the way to it and he alone knows where it dwells. God articulates the essence of wisdom, and to shun evil is understanding(28:28). That is the message of the Book of Job.

Relative to the book's dating: "Scholars are unsure when this book was written, with the suggested dates ranging from patriarchal to post-exilic times. The early date is supported by the fact that Job performs priestly functions in relation to his family (1:5) and his friends (42:8-9), indicating that the

Levitical sacrificial system promulgated by the Mosaic law was not yet in place."[7]

In a sermon a few years ago, the very reverend Samuel G. Candler asked, why is Job even in the Bible? He reasoned that it is "because the authentic community of faith, in this case, the Hebrew community of faith, acknowledged that innocent suffering does exist. Job represents innocent suffering. That suffering is authentic because it is not covered up, solved, or answered. . . . Moan or yell out to God! Your anger is evidence that you are in relationship."[8]

The Book of Job constitutes a critique and an implicit deepening and transformation of Israel's understanding of creation, covenant, and history. What does it mean to be the divine image and therein a royal figure on the earth? What does it mean to affirm simultaneously that to be human is to be dust and the royal image of God?

Consequently, Job's ash heap becomes his schoolroom with three friends as his supposed teachers. All Job can do is say nothing for seven days. Out of respect, his friends keep quiet also, waiting until Job speaks out of his misery. Total silence is not just the order of the day; it is the compelling force that wells up in Job's soul and cancels out any ability to make conversation. "Misery on steroids" might be one way to describe his existential crisis! He can utter no fitting words. His pain and disease aren't verbalized through his vocal cords but are validated more powerfully in the loss of his will to speak. Job's silent pitifulness delays his lament, and eventually, he hurls a barrage of questions at God to the tune of "Why me?"

After hearing Job wondering out loud why he was even born, the three friends initially seek to provide some semblance of comfort. However, they functionally each fill the role of his accusers, antagonists, or his nemeses. Job's three friends are Eliphaz the Temanite, Bildad the Shuhite, and Zophar the Naamathite. The fact that they had heard of Job's situation from their separate tribal areas amplifies the fact that Job's travails had reached far and wide across tribal lands. Although each is from a different tribe, they evidently had a common religion that enabled them to converse with each other religiously while contradicting Job's theological stances at every turn.

Job is immediately put at odds with his friends because he sees God as the cause of his suffering—while deserving nothing of the kind—and his "friends" don't. Job's friends clearly assume that, instead, it is Job's own sins that have caused his suffering and loss. Within their belief systems, they cannot theologically balance Job's debilitating health condition along with the tremendous losses of his grown children, servants, and livestock with the idea that Job says he has not sinned. Within their religious tradition, this would not seem possible. Interestingly, this does not prevent them from staying with Job for seven days. However, the friends seem to believe in a transactional relationship with the Divine: you do good, you get blessed, but your sins will be punished. Eliphaz, Bildad, and Zophar's beliefs are that God afflicts the sinful and blesses the sinless, which is not a status they can even claim for themselves. As theologian Christian Duquoc says, "We must note that in the dialogue sections it is not suffering as such which causes Job to rebel, but what the friends say."[9]

Having heard of Job's uncommon and unpleasant afflictions, his three friends couldn't even look at him upon their arrival at the ash heap. Traumatic pain doesn't just hurt, it distorts. Trauma not only disturbs our minds and emotions, to some degree, it can transfigure our appearance. As Job scraped his pus-filled sores and writhed in pain, his soul was raw and ready to react to any blame or bad news. Such physical discomfort, coupled with his emotional and spiritual anguish, pulsates through his many questions with a "Why me?" undertow. As Christian Duquoc offers, "Job has spoken correctly of God (which) means that Job still clung to the God whom he experienced as his adversary . . . This is the solution to the two faces of Job. The pious, humble man, submissive to God's will, and the desperate man who resists God—these are one and the same person, in touch with both possibilities."[10]

Through three cycles of speeches, Eliphaz, Bildad, and Zophar aim at comforting Job. Within these speeches, which I will discuss more thoroughly in chapter 4, Job's friends provide significantly more accusations than comfort. Wrestling with these accusations ignites a heartbreaking and irrational firestorm within Job. He lobs 150-plus questions at them and at God in his attempt to unearth some reason for his dilemma.

Perhaps after our personal experiences of trauma or some significant loss, setback, or devastating illness, we, too, might prefer silence over speeches. These friends are ready to debate all aspects of their faith and relationship with God, believing that they are better theologians than Job ever thought he could be. Their objectivity is minimal as they blame Job for all that has befallen him, leaving no subjective stone unturned. They believe they are helping him in their attempts to penetrate his denials about his sins. Their theology allows for a retributive relationship with God, and Job's does not, which seemingly pushes Job toward a primal scream or two as a coping mechanism for the pain of his physical, psychological, emotional, and spiritual struggles, given the depth of his despair and his sense of being mistreated. We cannot always count on our friends to understand the complexities of our situations or how we react to them. But sometimes such friends just cannot keep quiet nor allow us to fully react out of the depths of our humanity.

Job's religious observations offer him minimal comfort. Per his customs, he shaves his head in grief and tosses ashes heavenward as a prayer. Then he places himself on the ash heap in sorrow, repentance, and isolation. Journey with me into the depths of Job's reactions. Job's questions emerge not just from his sense of wonder, but from the friends' accusations that target the need in his very soul's struggle to make peace with his God.

Except for his wife, everything else in which he might find joy and meaning is gone. The loss of his children and everything he owned that had qualified him to be touted among the wealthiest people in the East had simply evaporated in the blink of an eye. He had no goodbyes, not a kiss or a hug from his children. As their father and priest, it was his joy to offer sacrifices to God in case they had sinned.

Eliphaz speaks first, challenging Job with these words:

> Will you be patient and let me say a word?
> For who could keep from speaking out?
>
> In the past you have encouraged many people;
> you have strengthened those who were weak.
> Your words have supported those who were falling;
> you encouraged those with shaky knees.
> But now when trouble strikes, you lose heart.
> You are terrified when it touches you.
> Doesn't your reverence for God give you confidence?
> Doesn't your life of integrity give you hope?
>
> (4:1-8, NLT)

Eliphaz initially praises Job for all the good he has done, but then he chides Job for recoiling from his own suffering. He is like a friend who immediately weeps with you in sorrow after hearing of your misfortune and then wonders out loud, "But what did you do . . . ?" once he discovers how devastating the situation is. Eliphaz found consoling words hard to come by. His presence was the only offering he could bring during those initial seven days with Job.

We've all been there: death of a loved one, marital breakup, loss of your job, a storm that destroys the home you love and upon which you lavish the wealth of your time and treasure, or some other crisis. Oftentimes no words can reach into the depths of what we are feeling after experiencing such tragic moments. We, then, begin conversations within ourselves, with God, and eventually with those who come to comfort us as we verbalize the question, "Why me?"

Job eventually journeys from that painful question, "Why me?" to "Why *not* me?" When we ask the first question, we may be excluding ourselves from the rest of humanity, believing ourselves to be not only *an* exception but *the* exemption from the rest of humanity. The second question recognizes that no humans are exempt from some experience of pain or trauma, disappointments, or cataclysmic moments from which we cannot escape! Though pain is costly in so many ways, there is significant evidence that the very experience of it can be our wisest, if not our greatest, teacher. Sadly, like Job, we have no how-to manuals to read in the throes of our personal despair that could help us cope a bit better or provide some answers to us in such devastating moments.

Within my years of ministry and counseling others, I have discerned that perhaps the most profound and maybe the most frequent questions humans ask are "Why?" or "Why me?" Even across a variety of cultures, these two questions seem to permeate the human lived experience. We seek solutions that often neither resolve our problems nor satisfy us. Sometimes our proposed solutions even fail to improve our situation or outlook. That is not a failure of our sources. All sources except for the Creator are limited in scope and depth to craft an appropriate or needed answer. This biblical book, as it presents the person of Job, provides a transcultural, religious, human profile as to the source in whom answers to these two questions are usually found. Our "Why?" and "Why me?" questions are not just questions of self-pity or existential angst; they significantly buttress our self-identity in comparison to others. And such answers usually satisfy more than our minds. They go far deeper, framing, shaping, fortifying, or perhaps even diminishing one's sense of self. Psychologists identify that task as the tenacious work of the ego.

The ego is a natural source of the pain we experience, which gives rise to the agonizing "Why me?" as we negotiate our path through and beyond the trauma we are experiencing. Because we may feel secure in who we are, at a very deep level, we *know* that it—good or bad—is not supposed to happen to us but to others, believing that we possibly have neither earned nor deserved what has happened to us.

No wonder Job had to sit by himself in a place he had not set before: an ash heap signifying a depth of pathos and undeserved suffering with which he could not reconcile himself. In Job's mind, based on his personal behaviors, he didn't deserve such catastrophes. From that ash heap, Job would not only wrestle with his friends, combating their accusations, but also with God, for whom Job had some disdain but mainly a deluge of questions. It is a time of untangling such inexplicable horrors and recapturing his sense of self and worth. Initially, there were no words—only the need for silence as Job initially sought in vain to "find" God. His soul explores the universe—east, west, north, south—but to no avail. He summed up his search in these poignant words:

> But if I go to the east, he is not there;
> if I go to the west, I do not find him.
> When he is at work in the north, I do not see him;
> when he turns to the south, I catch no glimpse of him.
> But he knows the way that I take;
> when he has tested me, I will come forth as gold. (23:8-10)

Job pays homage to the omniscient, sovereign knowledge of God. He recognizes that when we do not know where to find God, God easily knows how and where to find us. The external conversations recorded in this book probably cannot match the potency of Job's internal primal conversation and spiritual prayers simultaneously taking place. The struggle is not about Job simply being sad, angry, or even wrestling with God in his confusion, ignorance, or anger. It is about his letting go of the old reality—*how things were before his suffering began*—so he might gain a new sense of reality that has his name on it. God has not forgotten Job, and neither does God ever forget us, especially when we, like Job, have searched the four corners of creation and our very being to find the God who is already there.

Job sat in silence, but an explosive conversation was taking place in his mind, heart, and soul. His rhetoric was about to be unleashed in its full potency toward the friends who had sat in his presence in contradistinction to his God who seemed so far away. But before he could engage with them, he had this tiny annoying matter that would not let him go. He was wondering why, if he could not have been aborted, God allowed him to be born. Psychologically, that's such a negative reality of self—to wish that one could never have existed—but it is reflective of the pain of life.

In his first utterance, Job opened his mouth and cursed the fact that he had ever been born. But Job goes even further. He not only wishes he had never been born but also curses the very moment of his conception! "After this opened Job his mouth, and cursed his day. And Job spake, and said, Let the day perish wherein I was born, and the night in which it was said, There is a man child conceived" (3:1-3, KJV).

Take a moment and imagine the worst, most devastating moment of your life. Can you imagine yourself not only regretting the life you have but possibly even cursing the very moment you were conceived? Although clearly Job did not curse God, to have cursed his own moment of being conceived is coming as close as one can get, because only God determines any moment of conception.

Welcome to a new reality, Job! Welcome to a new birth. This birth, however, doesn't flush Job out of the womb of a nine-month cocooned space; rather, it welcomes Job into a space too wide for human comprehension. Often that space is too painful to endure and too enmeshed in contradictions about life for Job (or us) to even see the light of day. Nothing that happened to Job was on his list of possibilities. He was living the good life before being blindsided by the two tests Satan requested and God chose to allow—all of which were far worse than Job could ever imagine. Silence is not just Job's coping mechanism; it is his personal preparation for battle with the God he thought he knew and served. Job begins to mentally reconfigure his life.

The best metaphor with which he can frame his situation is the interplay of light and darkness. For him, light and darkness become symbols of good and evil. With that, he seeks to recreate his own journey, which you will soon discover is a spectacular interplay of light and darkness! This journey helps him to grasp a faith that was yet quite nascent if existent at all. In my personal study, I noticed that the greatest number of times "light" appears in the Bible is in the Book of Job, along with the second largest number of times that "darkness" appears. God is staging Job's life through these dynamic opposites. Other great historical leaders such as Mahatma Gandhi have noted such contrasts. After his 250-mile Salt March in India, Gandi traveled to England where he delivered what he called a "spiritual message" at the famous Kingsley Hall in London. No doubt, caught within the darkness of British oppression of his native India, he knew the power of light to them in their fight for liberation. He declared that he saw God "as purely benevolent, for I can see that in the midst of death life persists, in the midst of untruth truth persists, in the midst of darkness light persists. Hence, I gather that God is life, truth, light. He is love . . . God to be God must rule the heart and transform it."[11] What wondrous hope that sentiment conveys, and perhaps Gandhi's words reflect the potentially powerful spiritual transformation already underway in the mind, heart, and life of Job.

Darkness defines Job's soul while light defines his vanishing hopes. He asks in 3:20, "Why is light given to those in misery?" In his deep sense of powerlessness, Job sees no need for light because no perceivable goodness remains within his existence. And yet he longs for it. He believes that light succumbs to darkness since he saw no other way to express the agony he was experiencing in his body, his life, his status, and his very soul. Neither light nor darkness alone could provide any gratification to Job at that moment. He felt as if death was his only hope to ever see light again. Death could become his passage out of the darkness that was so very traumatizing. Such words further reveal how raw and how upended his life was and how devastating his losses had been.

The powerless feeling left Job unable to respond to his visiting friends for rebuking his beliefs and diminishing him in the process. He knows, of course, that they are not the ones perpetrating his seeming demise or the devastation he is experiencing. Feeling that his life is ebbing away without him having power to stop it, he nevertheless can see that light is not far away: "My days have passed, my plans are shattered. Yet the desires of my heart turn night into day; in the face of the darkness light is near" (17:11-12).

Nothing Job's friends say works to console him or bring any relief to the anguish in his body, mind, or soul. Rather, those friends choose to verbally spar with him instead. As we will see in their speeches, they relentlessly accuse Job of having sinned. Otherwise, they wonder out loud, would God allow such evils to befall him? Their words are empty of reality and powerless to convince Job that his problem is sin, and consequently, Job cannot deny being deserving of everything that has happened to him. They are comfortless comforters indeed! Thus, they continue to be naysayers, ushering in shades of darkness for Job that inhibit the light for which he so desperately seeks. While perceiving God as his enemy toward whom he can only hurl his vain and violent questions like a blind boxer, Job is closer to the light that he hopes for than he could possibly imagine. Like Job, often our answer(s) are just beyond our darkest hour.

With his questions, Job continues to climb out of his quicksand of pity and onto a path that leads toward hope, which eventually transforms his suffering inquiries from "Why me?" to "Why not me?" Job alters his search for the reason

God even cares: "What is mankind that you make so much of them, that you give them so much attention?" (7:17).

As Job works his way through his doubts, he begins to see the trees from the forest. That the humanity of which he is a part is greater than the idiosyncratic strife that defines his life. And to Zophar, in defense of his ego, Job bellows, "I have a mind as well as you; I am not inferior to you" (12:3). "Which of all these [animals of creation] does not know that the hand of the LORD has done this? In his hand is the life of every creature and the breath of all mankind" (12:9-10). After acknowledging their common human status, Job continues to validate his friends' humanity and his own as well.

The tragedy of pitying ourselves to the extreme is that it mentally, emotionally, or spiritually removes us from our human lot of identifying with other human beings. When we do this, we make ourselves the exception, which serves to deepen our sorrow rather than eliminating, minimizing, or allowing us to emerge out of it. The "Why me?" syndrome makes us, like Job, isolate ourselves from others which inhibits their ability to console us. It neglects the fact that when it comes to experiencing misfortunes, no one is the exception.

And we, too, bear a little less pain when we choose not to project our suffering as something beyond the experience of the rest of humanity. Our personal pity parties may leave us believing that we are alone in what we are experiencing. Isolating ourselves and feeling undeserving not only makes a profound psychological difference but negatively impacts the quality of our spiritual lives. Our faith and trust in God can assure us that if God has not forgotten all of humanity, then neither has God forgotten us in our plight. Job's friends continue to increase their sense of religious superiority over Job, believing they know God better than he does. While accusing him of great sins, they are unaware of their own sins in boldly othering the very soul they came to comfort. They are enjoying their own self-exalted state while diminishing Job's value in their own eyes.

In the next chapter, we will take a deeper look at the role of Job's friends in his struggles. Before we do so, I invite you to pause for reflection on the following questions.

Questions for Reflection and/or Response

1. How have we responded to some of our most traumatic moments in life personally, locally, or globally?
2. Where is your place of silence—like Job's ash heap—where you can go to make sense of your circumstances? What makes your place of silence special and healing?
3. What's at the root of the question, "Why me?" when we are in difficult circumstances or overwhelmed? In what ways does your question, "Why me?" impact your faith or your relationship with Christ?
4. Amazingly, Job cursed his life, birth, and conception. Identify times when you have "cursed" aspects of your life. What questions do you ask God when you are frustrated or unable to change a challenging situation in your life?

Notes

1. Stephen J. Vicchio, *The Voice from the Whirlwind: The Problem of Evil and the Modern World* (Maryland: Christian Classics, 1989), 125.
2. "One considered by members of a dominant group as alien, exotic, threatening, or inferior . . . because of different racial, sexual, or cultural characteristics." Merriam-Webster online, s.v. "othering."
3. Harold S. Kushner, *The Book of Job: When Bad Things Happened to a Good Person*, Jewish Encounters Series (New York: Random House, 2012), 7–8.
4. Norman C. Habel, *The Book of Job* (Cambridge, England: Cambridge University Press, 2008).
5. Abraham Joshua Heschel, *Man Is Not Alone: A Philosophy of Religion* (New York: Noonday Press, 1951), 13.
6. Tokunboh Adeyemo, ed., *Africa Bible Commentary* (Grand Rapids: Zondervan, 2006), 571.
7. Tokunboh Adeyemo, ed., *Africa Bible Commentary* (Grand Rapids: Zondervan, 2006), 572.
8. Samuel G. Candler, "Why Is the Book of Job Even in the Bible?" October 22, 2018, https://www.cathedralatl.org/goodfaithpostings/why-is-the-book-of-job-even-in-the-bible/#:.

9. Christian Duquoc et al., eds., *Concilium: Job and the Silence of God* (New York: Seabury, 1983), 22.
10. Ibid., 21.
11. NDTV Correspondent. 2011. "Mahatma Gandhi's famous speech at Kingsley Hall in 1931," October 3, 2011. https://www.ndtv.com/india-news/mahatma-gandhis-famous-speech-at-kingsley-hall-in-1931-565204

Chapter Four

WITH FRIENDS LIKE THESE . . .

When Job's friends Eliphaz the Temanite, Bildad the Shuhite, and Zophar the Naamathite hear of his suffering, they want to comfort him. Eliphaz arrives from the south and is thought to be the chief Teman mentioned in Genesis 36:42, who possibly bequeathed his name to his progeny. The Temanites, mentioned four times by the prophets, are possibly a subtribe of the Edomites. Bildad the Shuhite is not the first Shuhite mentioned in Scripture. His name has a more reverential meaning: "brought low" or "prostration." The first Shuah (שוח; pronounced *shuach*) is mentioned as a son of Abraham with Keturah in Genesis 25:2. Zophar the Naamathite is from Naamath (Naamah; נעמה), a town in Judah. The only one in the Bible, his name is listed under the verb נעם (*na'em*), meaning "to be pleasant," and he hails from the west.[1]

As they arrive and see Job from a distance, the friends barely recognize him. Wailing loudly, the friends tear their robes and throw dust into the air over their heads, expressing their grief. The Hebrew tradition of rending one's clothing as a sign of grief is called *keriah*.[2] Although these are friends and not family, their actions symbolize the deep sense of empathy they feel toward Job. They can hardly bear sitting on the ground around Job and his ash heap for seven days and nights. Seeing that Job's suffering is too great for words, silence prevails.

In Job's first silence-breaking speech, words pour out with volcanic velocity, cursing or disdaining seemingly everything but God. That list includes not only Job's birth but darkness, light, the morning stars, and even daylight! Nothing seems safe from Job's prevailing pain and bitterness. His friends cannot lessen the pain and discomfort Job is feeling nor assuage his wish for death. Having accused God of hedging him in, Job sets his sights on that place where "the wicked cease from troubling, and . . . the weary are at rest" (3:17, RSV).

In Job's mind, all other possibilities are as exhausted as he feels in his body and spirit. Then his friends verbally seize on him, having heard him blame God for his condition, as demonstrated in chapters 4-5, 11, and 18, as well as others. To the friends, Job's theological explanations are faulty, which vaporizes any comfort they might offer. Blame comes fast. Their egos allow them to challenge Job's theology while reveling in their self-superior religious attitudes. And so, the debate begins.

Job's friends initially display empathy and respect, which seem deep and abiding. But they quickly abandon this approach after listening to Job's complaints. Their presence is no longer a source of comfort and consolation. When the friends do eventually speak, however, their utter confusion about the source of and reason for Job's suffering such affliction becomes an additional source of pain for Job. They seize on the opportunity to share their religious beliefs as a basis for their immediate assessment of Job's problem. They choose to devalue or *other* Job, trusting that their beliefs and knowledge of God are superior to his. So quickly they allow that chasm of difference to be filled with contempt and loathing.

Othering in the Bible

A dear friend recently asked me, "What does the Bible, or Job, teach us about *othering*? Is there something in Job that we can learn from to eradicate the need for othering?" I believe that much of the conflict between people and a great source of trauma comes through othering or seeing others as something different and something to shun, change, or conquer. While the use of the word othering may seem recent, I conclude that the act of othering humans is as old as humanity itself. Sadly, we see evidence of it in the Bible even here in the Book of Job. Job and his friends not only differ theologically but spar with each other around the quality of their knowledge, and subsequently, strongly other or devalue one another in the process. That realization astounded me because it not only added more texture to their relationships but provided a new connection to twenty-first-century culture as well. Here are a few examples I gleaned from their initial sparing:

From Bildad: "If you're as innocent and upright as you say, it's not too late. . . . Even though you're not much right now, you'll end up better than ever" (8:6-7, MSG).

From Eliphaz: "When desperate people give up on God Almighty, their friends, at least, should stick with them. But my brothers are fickle as a gulch in the desert" (6:14-15, MSG).

From Zophar: "Job, do you think you can carry on like this and we'll say nothing? That we'll let you rail and mock and not step in? You claim, 'My doctrine is sound and my conduct impeccable.' How I wish God would give you a piece of his mind, tell you what's what!" (11:3-5, MSG).

Within these speeches, a dynamic tension exists between Job's spiritual quest and his friends' theological beliefs. While they disagree about dogma on one level, they validate Job's quest for God on another level. In this conversation, Job expects comfort, but these friends bring doubt, conflict, and othering to disparage Job and add weight to their self-justifications. This intensifies the exchanges with Job and fuels his barrage of questions, nudging and leading him toward his ultimate repentance, renewal, and restoration.

Legitimate Questions

I believe these friends were pushing Job to answer four valid questions:

> Who am I in relation to . . . ?
> What do I know of God?
> What do I believe about God?
> What do I do as a consequence of what I know and believe?

These questions helped me to perceive what I identify as the *Job paradigm*, which is a definitive pattern and process of spiritual growth, particularly during a crisis. It is a window that allows a reader to peer within the life of a religious person's faith journey. Job not only sees himself as a victim, but he is also revealed to be in the depths of despair, self-pitying, and wishing for an honorable means of exiting this life, to the point of cursing his birth and even the very moment of his conception.

Eliphaz, the first friend to address Job, initially encourages Job to stop feeling sorry for himself, even praising him for the good he had often done for others. He later spurts out: "Can a mortal be more righteous than God? Can even a strong man be more pure than his Maker?" (4:17). The question seems far more accusatory than rhetorical because he also reminds Job that he is just like everybody else. He also chides him for not blaming fate when troubles come his way: "Evil does not spring from the soil, and trouble does not sprout from the earth. People are born for trouble as readily as sparks fly up from a fire" (5:6-7, NLT). Convinced of Job's sinfulness, Eliphaz advises, "If I were you, I would appeal to God; I would lay my cause before him" (5:8). In other words, evil is in you, buddy, and that is why you are reaping all this suffering! Often, the words that follow such harsh condemnation are words of self-aggrandizement, that is, language that lets the speaker feel superior to the listener. And Eliphaz's words do just that: he seeks to increase his own influence and importance along with that of his other friends. While they push Job toward a greater sense of piety, they also seek more influence and power over him. Their sense of self-importance rises significantly now that they see Job's actual circumstance and condition; consequently, they reduce Job from friend to religious foe. Eliphaz, after preaching to Job, chides him to "hear it and apply it to yourself" (5:27). In his second speech, Eliphaz excoriates Job by saying, "[The godless] conceive trouble and give birth to evil; their womb fashions deceit" (15:35).

Don't be fooled by the word *friends*, which is used to describe these three who have come from afar to comfort Job. Although comfort was their original intent, after seeing him and sitting in silence with him for seven days, and then listening to his explanations, their understanding of his situation changed dramatically. They suddenly prefer to think of themselves as Job's teachers or theologians as opposed to his comforters or friends. Seeing Job's suffering and affliction, they cannot abide listening to him so vehemently declare his innocence. After all, they also know God. Consequently, their verbiage changes dramatically in both substance and tone. I have found that at times friends derive more of their understanding of one's situation from *projection* than from *detection*. Sometimes, even the best friends tend to reason about your circumstance out of what they have experienced rather than seeking sufficient details about your personal troubles. And that certainly seems to be the case with these friends.

But let us be clear—Job did not invite them. Job did not expect anyone to show up in his moment of diabolical trauma and tribulation. But as well-known as he was and as many lives were affected by the deaths of his children and workers, surely somebody was bound to show up and commiserate with him. Job just did not necessarily expect it to be these three, or for these three to so sadly denigrate him. They are initially friends who care, but their perception of Job is drastically catalyzed, making them chide, disbelieve, and condemn the very one they came to comfort. These friends cannot believe Job is being truthful about his life. To them, his sins are as evident as his sores. So why deny them? In their perception, hidden sin could be the only causal factor for Job's calamities. But Job is not dependent on their observations nor their diagnosis of his suffering. With a continuing barrage of questions, with no sin looming in his background, Job waits for God to answer.

This initial round of speeches challenges and confuses Job. It is theologically limited since the friends can only declare that in their understanding of a transactional relationship with God, Job deserves what has befallen him: *you sin, you get zonked!* Their best advice: *confess!* They prove to be great friends but render bad advice. Job's friends are quite religious. They believe they have a strong moral code to which they can hold Job accountable. They have their theory of justice and plenty of religious information about God but seemingly little experience relating to God. They have theories and thoughts but are devoid of wisdom that comes from God alone as evidence of a relationship born of love and trust. These friends relentlessly browbeat Job with their religious whip because of the sins they believe he has committed. Job finds no comfort in their accusations after being so meticulous about offering sacrifices for himself and his family members just in case he or they sinned against God. But that is insufficient for these friends. They believe Job must be hiding something; otherwise, God would not have allowed such traumatic events to befall him and his family.

Eliphaz's Advice (Chapters 4, 5, 15, 22)

Eliphaz opens the first of his three speeches very cautiously and with great respect for Job, citing the numerous times the tables were turned when Job counseled others. He remembers that Job even "encouraged those who were about to quit . . . [and even] put fresh hope in people about to collapse" (4:2-3, MSG). However, it does not take Eliphaz long to hit Job with a barrage of questions disparaging his so-called devout and exemplary life and concluding with the epithet, "Those who sow trouble reap it" (4:8). In essence, he's asking, "Are you more righteous than God?"

Job's plight is the result of the hand of almighty God and no one else, says Eliphaz. God wounds, Eliphaz declares, but God also dresses the wound. Perhaps Eliphaz is seasoning this diatribe with a bit of grace and hope for Job. For Eliphaz and the other friends, Job's disasters would be a flagrant disaster in their worldview and moral system. As a result, they become quite defensive as they cling to their own personal moral dogma.

Even good folks can spout the worst counsel when attempting to console others. After forty-one years, I find it painful to remember the moment at my mother's wake when one of my aunts, attempting to console me, thought of everyone else but me when she advised that I "needed to be strong for the rest of us!" In that moment, it felt more like she hated me, though all my life she had been one of the closest aunties. I deserved to have my moments to cry, wail, and even scream if need be with my mother having been taken from me so suddenly. My aunt seemingly wanted that only for herself and others but not for her sister's youngest child. Many church folk tend to diminish the humanity of their pastors or church leaders when something catastrophic happens to them, choosing instead to limit the amount of pain, anguish, or grief they want to see. Job had a strong track record of caring for others, which allowed Eliphaz, especially, to assume that Job could sufficiently minister to himself without falling apart. His comparison is faulty for many reasons, especially realizing that people do not experience trauma equally even in similar circumstances.

Bildad's Counsel (Chapters 8, 18, 25)

Bildad chimes in, accusing Job of talking nonsense, beginning with the question, *Does God mess up?* Then he advises Job, "Get down on your knees before God Almighty. If you're as innocent and upright as you say, it's not too late—he'll come running; he'll set everything right again, reestablish your fortunes" (8:5-6, MSG). He thinks that Job can learn from the ancestors, declaring that by comparison, "we're new at this" (8:9, MSG). But like many religious folks, moored in the world they can see, Bildad has a transactional concept of the human-divine relationship, "There's no way that God will reject a good person, and there is no way he'll help a bad one" (8:20, MSG). No matter the degree to which Job protests, he links Job in with the "God ignorant."

Like many folks in our Christian congregations, Job and Bildad are more entrenched in a historical religion than liberated into biblical faith that is clearly not a tit-for-tat transactional relationship, but one in which tragedies are not caused in our lives by a vengeful God and neither are our blessings rewards for good behavior. As the apostle Paul claims, faith is our victory *in trouble*, giving every believer bragging rights on God's grace in times of trouble, allowing wearied souls to triumph:

> Therefore, since we have been justified through faith, we have peace with God through our Lord Jesus Christ, through whom we have gained access by faith into this grace in which we now stand. And we boast in the hope of the glory of God. Not only so, but we also glory in our sufferings, because we

> know that suffering produces perseverance; perseverance, character; and character, hope. And hope does not put us to shame, because God's love has been poured out into our hearts through the Holy Spirit, who has been given to us. (Romans 5:1-5)

Too often we might think we know better than the person whose life has been uprooted by a storm of one kind or another. That is seldom, if ever, true! Though offered in good faith and a sense of caring, we are always only standing on the perimeter of someone else's life while their pain and eventual decisions are driven by internal and deeply personal sources.

Zophar's Wisdom (Chapters 11, 20)

Not to be out-done, Zophar says to Job,

> How I wish God would give you a piece of his mind,
> tell you what's what!
> I wish he'd show you how wisdom looks from the inside,
> for true wisdom is mostly "inside."
> But you can be sure of this,
> you haven't gotten half of what you deserve.
>
> —11:5-6 (MSG)

At least Zophar is aware that God, not Job's ancestors, is the source of wisdom. Though ancestors can leave a legacy of great advice in situations that later generations face, that advice is generated from their practical, lived experience in *their* time. Zophar posits that it is wisdom from the outside, not the inside, that belongs to and is given by God alone.

When they enter the second round of speeches, Zophar is incredulous about what he has heard from Job thus far. In fact, Zophar said to Job, "You've put my teeth on edge, my stomach in a knot. How dare you insult my intelligence like this!" (20:2-3). Blasting Job further because of the abundance of sins he believes Job must have committed to justify God's heaping loads of punishment and suffering upon Job, Zophar spews another layer of condemnation on sinners like Job:

> "God will strip them of their sin-soaked clothes
> and hang their dirty laundry out for all to see.
> Life is a complete wipeout for them,
> nothing surviving God's wrath.
> There! That's God's blueprint for the wicked—
> what they have to look forward to."
>
> —20:27 (MSG)

Zophar seems to be a perfect example of today's popular truism: "Hurting folks hurt folks." He appears to be full of venom and ready to attack his victim at the least provocation. Although he is aware of Job's standing in his community, Zophar doesn't live in close enough proximity to be familiar with Job's daily behavior, including all the sins he believes Job is hiding and refuses to confess to his friends or to God. From Zophar's religious perspective, he projects what he believes is God's vengeance against Job as evidence of Job's sinful behavior.

Anytime there is something like a divorce within the church family, someone's child going astray, a major car accident, or someone's house being destroyed, church gossipers launch into their gossip mill with comments like:

> "You know God don't like ugly."
> "And I thought she was supposed to be such a good wife."
> "They just let that child run wild."
> "They act like they so holy; looks like God don't think so."
> "Girl, let me tell you what I heard. . . ."
> "You know God ain't gonna let *that* pass."

They only see guilt, not grace—a vengeful God, not faith or hope. Much to our dismay, they often revel in malice, not mercy. While thinking of themselves as being holy and "right with God," they struggle to allow the same for another struggling believer. It makes you wonder at times, what in the world is *their* faith built on?

Guilty until Proven Innocent?

Job's friends Eliphaz, Bildad, and Zophar stopped answering Job because they perceived he was righteous in his own eyes (32:1). After describing Eliphaz, Bildad, and Zophar as impotent, Job declares that he would never deny his integrity and will maintain his innocence. He said, "My conscience will not reproach me as long as I live" (27:6).

Job's Reaction

Then Job reminisces about his good ole days when he felt that God really watched over him—that though he walked through darkness, God provided light for him. He describes those times before calamity struck as golden years when he experienced a sense of friendship with God. Job longs for days past when he was revered and celebrated in the city, at the city gate, and in his community. He thinks about the times when he not only had something to say but when both young and old folks listened to him (29:21-23). Job remembers the times before his suffering eclipsed his expectation of a long and fruitful life. He recalls when his speaking quieted the angst in those who listened, despite the responses of his three "friends" whose minds were pricked and whose attitudes waxed cold and harsh against him. Job considers himself a leader, declaring in essence, "Where I led, they followed."

Like Job's friends, it isn't always easy for us to discern within a conversation whether another person is somewhat religious, is not religious at all, or has a deeply religious or spiritual commitment. When we step into the moment of witnessing and bearing with someone's loss and suffering, we have no easily discernible way to perceive the depth or quality of their beliefs. And it is certainly not the time to probe their worldview or question their faith. We should never feel so self-righteous that we laud our relationship with God over others' relationships with him. Though parents might fail miserably in loving each child equally, God never does. No doubt our faith is a weapon, but it is for defensive tactics. Such precious faith is for our protection and sometimes for our own defense. Faith is never to be weaponized against others to diminish them in such ways as demonstrated by Job's friends.

While Job's friends compound his suffering, their questions may encourage Job to voice his own questions to God. In part as Job's rebuttal to Eliphaz, Bildad, and Zophar, Job creates a list of things he has never done nor would ever consider doing. In chapter 27, his preamble to his list of denials declares:

> As long as I have life within me,
> the breath of God in my nostrils,
> my lips will not say anything wicked,
> and my tongue will not utter lies.
> I will never admit you are in the right;
> till I die, I will not deny my integrity.
> I will maintain my innocence and never let go of it;
> my conscience will not reproach me as long as I live.
>
> —verses 3-6

The evidence of Job's righteous behavior is offered in chapter 31, which chronicles the basic expectations of a person who reveres God and who seeks to be faithful to God. I have chosen to paraphrase some of Job's denials in his effort to prove both his innocence and his reverence for God:

> I have not been deceitful. Even God knows I am blameless. My heart has not been led by my eyes. My heart has not been enticed by a woman. I have not lurked at my neighbor's door. I have not denied justice to any of my servants whether male or female. I have not denied the desires of the poor or the weary widow. I have not kept bread to myself. I have not let anyone perish for lack of clothing. I have not raised my hand against the fatherless. I have not made gold my security. I have not rejoiced at my enemy's misfortune or gloated over his troubles. No stranger has ever spent the night in the street, for my door was always open to the traveler. I have no guilt in my heart.

Because of Job's reverence for God as well as God's majesty and highness, Job says, "I could not do such things" (31:23). As he calls for God to answer him, he feels that he only needs someone to hear him as he concludes his rebuttal to Eliphaz, Bildad, and Zophar. Often the greater need in our protestations is just for someone to *hear* our side of the story.

Lessons in Waiting on God

For Job in his hour of need, it seemed as if God could not come fast enough. Honestly, his friends were not making the wait seem any shorter. While folks have long lauded Job for his supposed "patience" because they perceive him as idly waiting on God, describing it as patience is probably not entirely accurate. In his time of waiting, Job hurls scads of questions and some accusations at God while challenging the claims of his friends. Job says, "Be so kind as to look at me. Would I lie to your face?" (6:28). He asks that they stop assuming his guilt and continues to claim that he has done no wrong.

Job is not sitting idly under the barrage of accusations from these friends, nor is he waiting silently on God. His defensive posture toward his friends and toward God strongly suggests that he is far more impatient than patient. He does not wait for an answer to one question before another one flies like an arrow from his quiver of pain. Sitting on his ash heap, Job incessantly hurls questions horizontally and vertically—toward humans and heaven. These questions could even be characterized as demands. Job is a bit disdainful while pressing God to intervene. He remains relentless in his need to see God, and he uses questions to acquire God's attention. Neither his mind nor his soul can wait for answers, so each new question serves as a knock on heaven's door to make his plight plain. As I declared in my doctoral dissertation, "Job knows that he is known by God and that he knows God. Mature faith accomplishes greater balance between the two."[3]

Waiting on God is a biblical virtue. Psalm 37:7 exhorts, "Be still before the LORD and wait patiently for him." Lamentations 3:25-26 assures us that "The LORD is good to those whose hope is in him, to the one who seeks him; it is good to wait quietly for the salvation of the LORD." But *how* we wait is the real issue. Do we wait in faith? In doubt? Passively? No—we must wait actively and expectantly, trusting that God has not only heard our cry but also knowing that God will show up in God's time. That trust depends on whether we have a viable relationship with God. Having read about God or even achieving theological degrees is insufficient to establish such a relationship. To know that God is love and to trust God is never a merely academic endeavor.

Within Christian theology, we understand God as a God in relationship through the personages of the Father, the Son, and the Holy Spirit. God is not a single entity but a triune God. God requires our love and our trust, which sustains our hope! We cannot just *think* God, empowered by the abundance of information we have heard, perused, or studied. Though we must have information about God, the path to God is paved with love, trust, and commitment to God's values with helpful theological information being gleaned along the way.

Though such assurances came hundreds of years later, the Job story assures us that it is God who is indeed good to those who wait for God, although their perceived time of need may not be God's appointed time of deliverance. Even when such times are forced upon us and solutions to our sorrows seem out of our reach, we too often sit in a state of powerlessness raising questions that have no answers. Such moments are not empty but are pregnant with possibilities yet to be revealed! Because in our life of faith, Isaiah 30:18c (NIV) confirms, "Blessed are those who wait for God."

We have examined a sample of the ways Job's three friends may have challenged Job as he waited on the Lord. The words and actions of Job's friends can tell us much about how our presence may inform the faith development of others, whether for good or bad. In the next chapter, we will deeply discuss what the Book of Job tells us regarding wisdom. Before we do so, I invite you to pause and reflect on the following questions.

Questions for Reflection and/or Response

1. What makes these seemingly obnoxious friends almost irrelevant or not? Explain.
2. In trying circumstances, what do you need most from your spiritual tools?
3. Why might our spiritual tools (e.g., prayer, meditation, Bible reading) not necessarily feel helpful to others in stressful experiences?
4. What does it mean to have a transactional relationship with others? With God?
5. What is the opposite of othering, and how can you avoid making others feel as if they do not belong to the same group that you do?
6. What does it feel like when others weaponize their faith against you? How might you respond?

7. How do you strengthen and encourage your faith when being attacked or belittled by others?

Notes

1. "Zophar Meaning," Abarim Publications, accessed June 3, 2023, https://www.abarim-publications.com/Meaning/Zophar.html.
2. Maurice Lamm, "Keriah—The Rending of Garments," Chabad.org, accessed June 3, 2023, https://www.chabad.org/library/article_cdo/aid/281558/jewish/Keriah-The-Rending-of-Garments.htm#Who.
3. Paige Lanier Chargois, "Faith Development: The Job Paradigm, A Pastoral Model" (DMin diss., United Theological Seminary, 1994), 73.

Chapter Five

THROUGH WISDOM TO FAITH (Job 28)

How glorious it is to hear, recite, and even live by the wisdom of the ages, whether that wisdom is drawn from the biblical sayings attributed to Solomon or sayings from Aristotle, Aunt Sue, or Grandma. These people offer wisdom that has emerged from their lived-out years, from their mental calculations, or from their more profound reasoning capacities coupled with a good education. Such reasoning is not wrong from a biblical perspective or human standards and capacities—it is simply incomplete. Chapter 28 in the Book of Job is a meditation on wisdom. This chapter contains the only poetry in the book not attributed to a speaker. The meditation addresses what is, perhaps, the very reason for the book—to show and confirm the source of wisdom. No measure of human intellect or wisdom is sufficient without the divine dimension to guide and sustain us. Simply put: we need God.

Knowledge accumulated over the years can be helpful, but alone it is insufficient to supply the deeper answers for living that we often seek. Much wisdom that we claim in our lives can be characterized as just good advice that addresses practical situations or relational issues. What soothes our souls and offers greater confidence for most of us, however, is when advice or counsel is from a divine source. And that is what we see in the story of Job—he pursues answers from God that qualify as the very formation of his rational and spiritual being. Job is seeking his *raison d'être*, which helps him cope with the misfortune he is experiencing. Through pursuing God with scores of questions, he eventually receives the answers he needs albeit in the form of questions.

The answers God offers are implicit in the questions God hurls back at Job (see chapters 40 and 41). God's questions are filled with wisdom, helping to better tune Job's relationship with the Divine. The conversation between Job and God is not a friendly discussion by any means. Rather, it is an inquisition—the full use of semantic power from both human and divine dimensions. Job pursues wisdom with his 150-plus questions that help him make sense of his suffering. God's questions to Job ensured that Job could succeed in that quest.

Biblically, the source of wisdom is rarely to be found along the human spectrum; nor is it ever to be seen as synonymous with human intellect, scientific research, or accumulated experience. It is not attainable through human prowess or mental machinations. Wisdom, declares the Bible, comes solely from the Creator, whose power and knowledge span from creation through eternity. The prophets and writers of the so-called wisdom literature within Holy Writ declare this to be true. Proverbs 3:19 (NRSV) tells us, "The LORD by wisdom founded the earth; by understanding he established the heavens," and the prophet Jeremiah says, "It is [God] who made the earth by his power, who established the world by his wisdom" (10:12, NRSV).

Someone once expressed the thought that wisdom is not our human ability to preserve or extend our lives but rather to gain prowess in applying our lives to the variety of circumstances we encounter along our way. In contrast, the Greeks perceived wisdom (*sophia*) as derived from the human intellect and speculation. However, wisdom for the

Hebrews (*hokmah*) was subject to divine causes and sources but also included skill in practical matters and various areas of life. According to *The Theological Wordbook of the Old Testament*, "Hebrew wisdom was not theoretical and speculative. It was practical, based on revealed principles of right and wrong, to be lived out in daily life."[1] Job's reflection on wisdom aligns with the Hebrew understanding of the word.

Historically, many Westerners have considered wisdom to be indicative of one's ability to think great thoughts. Many perceive wisdom as the quality of one's cognitive ability, and we offer a variety of tests within our institutions and businesses to support that idea. We tend to think of the philosopher as being the opposite of the manual laborer of whatever craft. However, in Hebrew, the noun *hokmah* includes both when it comes to being wise. It is practical and applicable to this world, and not just otherworldly.

The Book of Job is classified as part of the collection of wisdom writings within the Bible, so we understand that it is intended to be instructive on wisdom. Although Job's words and behaviors do not always suggest any nascent learning, we recognize that this story illustrates how the quality of human cognitive wrestling informs wisdom. Our wrestling with questions enables our arrival at a level of human reality that both ensures and assures our fuller comprehension of life. It is because wisdom, like our breath, finds its source in God. As breath sustains our physical lives, divine wisdom provides strength and quality to that life.

Prior to his calamities, Job uttered the following: "Naked I came from my mother's womb, and naked shall I return there; the LORD gave, and the LORD has taken away; blessed be the name of the LORD" (1:21). He not only perceived the ultimate causal factor of his multiple calamities, but when he utters, "The LORD . . . ," Job reasons that somewhere within his hellacious experiences, a reason remains to worship God, praise God, and celebrate the divine connection with humans. Within what might seem like vacuous space to some lies the very seedbed of wisdom: the human ability to make rhyme and reason out of life itself.

Walter Brueggemann says, "The pragmatic approach seeks to come to terms with the nearly hidden order of God that must be embraced and accepted as the only viable context in which an effective, joyous, and secure life can be lived."[2] No doubt, God and God's dealings with Job are well hidden from Job at the human experiential end of those divine decisions and plans. The results of those dealings fully define the heinous realities that Job is experiencing: the death of his children, the death of his oxen and camels, the destruction of his properties, the painful boils on his body, and more.

Within his finite space, Job can find no human to hold accountable. So, he has to look beyond the merely human sphere toward the divine realm. Though he has neither authority nor power to hold God accountable, Job certainly trusts that God is reliable, which becomes the essence and the power of being in covenant with God. That is not faith itself; it's the initial human-divine connection out of which faith can flow and mature. Brueggemann also says that "wisdom teaching is creation theology, a reflection upon lived experience in an attempt to discern the regularities of life that are taken to be the ordering of reality that the creator God decreed and guaranteed."[3]

Job's mind is devoid of explanations about his situation, just as we are often incapable of neatly making sense of our own calamities. His soul finds such losses and suffering inexplicable. So, Job reaches toward the one whom he believes sustains his very life. Job commences fathoming some answers for his life. In so doing, he discovers the very source of wisdom itself. The three friends are just the opposite, becoming hardened toward Job. They are convinced of Job's sinfulness because of the adversities that undeniably plague his very existence. Their philosophy of life and religious convictions are quite simplistic. As Raymond Scheindlin reflects,

"Their purpose is consolation, and their means is an ancient wisdom . . . that posited an exact correlation between behavior and outcome: a good person will succeed, and a wicked person will eventually fail."[4]

The contrast between Job's beliefs and the beliefs of his friends is vivid and awesome. Job looks beyond human causal frailties not only for reasons but also for answers and a solution to such a disruption of his life. Time will show that the meeting of their minds becomes less and less possible as the rest of the friends' speeches candidly reveal. Thus, we have the human cauldron within which Job and his friends verbally spar over his recent calamities. Plus, they debate over one another's religious ideologies because of what God has permitted in Job's life. "Wisdom will die with you," Job spews toward Zophar in 12:1 (NRSV) after his first speech. But Eliphaz shoots right back at him: "Would a wise person answer with empty notions or fill their belly with the hot east wind? Would they argue with useless words, with speeches that have no value?" (15:1-3).

What does this interaction between Job and his friends reveal to us about our behavior when we face calamities? What source(s) of wisdom do we seek? What fund of knowledge do we bring to bear upon our situation? To what depth do we probe for an answer? How do we satisfy our human angst, anger, or anxiety? Various human sources may provide some seemingly effectual response or appropriate reaction that fits the moment. The Book of Job, however, suggests that only God has the answers to heal our lives and propel us toward the grand future God alone can offer us. Do we—or can we—discern the difference between wisdom and advice? We might often seek out advice from someone, but how often do we seek wisdom? Advice is an answer to a practical question, while wisdom is a more profound response to a deeper human need, compelling us to search deeper, to search for meaning beneath what is practical, physical, or efficient, for example:

> Question: "Which is the best restaurant in town?"
> Response: "Why do you need to go to the best?"
>
> Question: "Why have you chosen *that* job with low pay and few benefits?"
> Answer: "It's what I feel called to do."

Advice adds information to our lives, but wisdom adds meaning! Although advice can help and is needed, it cannot provide the strength and substance, clarity, or sense of purpose to our lives that wisdom can.

We go to friends. We go to medical doctors. We go to therapists. We go to family members. As informed and caring as they may be, human information can't compare with divine wisdom. Education and training (as well as longevity) can prove beneficial as sources of knowledge, but they are no match for the Source of wisdom. The compelling message of this biblical book is that we must find our way to God regardless of how circuitous that route might be. As for Job, and even Job's friends, some level of humility just might be necessary. It is not easy to humble ourselves before the God who invites us into the ring to spar with him. However, like Job's experience, we just might get pummeled into adoration with questions that allude not only to God's power to create but also to God's power over all of creation! "Do you send the lightning bolts on their way? Do they report to you, 'Here we are'?" (38:35). No! Or, "Does the eagle soar at your command?" (39:27). No! God asks unanswerable questions while leading Job toward the answers he is seeking. Such awareness moves us mere earthlings beyond simple explanations about our situation toward deeper questing: "Why me? Why not me?" Gaining such insights strengthens us for more fortuitous decisions yet to come. God's wisdom transcends any rationale that we might affix to the moral codes that shape our earthly existence.

Job clasps his hand over his mouth in regret and humble submission to God after recognizing that he is in the match of his life. He has met the Author of his existence and the Creator of his very soul who could season his life with the wisdom he needs. Job proclaims that he had previously only "heard about God," but now he is on his way to seeing God with his own eyes (42:5).

Indeed, God transcends that divine-human distance with Job when he answers Job's questions with questions of his own making. God could clearly provide Job with a new canvas for his life. This time it would be one on which the artistry of divine relationship is painted with the brushstrokes of faith.

The meditation on wisdom in the Book of Job contrasts the fact that we humans know where to find gold, silver, iron, copper, and even rock, "but where can wisdom be found? Where does understanding dwell? No mortal comprehends its worth; it cannot be found in the land of the living. . . . God understands the way to it, and he alone knows where it dwells" (28:12-13, 23). Wisdom is not to be valued like the rarest of minerals, nor can it be traded for jewels or trinkets. The *source* of wisdom is what we humans must seek. Though we know it exists, the source is hidden from human perception, and only God knows its domain. So, our personal, mental, and spiritual pursuit is to encounter God, to immerse ourselves in the substantive being he offers us. Within God, we discover the wisdom necessary for living our most productive and purposeful life. In God, we move beyond the superficial layers of life, which can allow us to be successful on some level and enjoy a relationship that provides strength beyond human capacities and a relationship with the Creator.

Some might think that the building blocks of our lived-out existence or even our relationship with God are not a series of questions; rather, they are answers that we need and long for. We can become very tired of questions being asked or of even asking them ourselves. But whether it is a scientist, a quizzical child, or simply a soul seeking solace, we all must learn to master the quality of our questions so that we can arrive at the answers that solve our situations. The reflection questions below may help you shape your big questions in life. After you work through them, I invite you to turn the page and be refreshed by the power of the questions life demands that we ask—sooner or later.

Questions for Reflection and/or Response

1. What are your strategic or go-to coping mechanisms?
2. How do you define wisdom and distinguish it from good advice?
3. What are some ways God infuses wisdom into our human situations?
4. How could Job say, "The LORD gave and the LORD has taken away; may the name of the LORD be praised" (1:21)? When have you said or thought similarly of the Lord as Job did? Explain.
5. Envision a couple of situations in which you might hesitate to ask God questions. Why? Where? Give an example.
6. Name a person in history to whom you would love to question how they made it through a challenging time. What made you choose that person?

Notes

1. R. Laird Harris, Gleason L. Archer Jr., Bruce K. Waltke, *Theological Wordbook of the Old Testament* (Chicago: Moody, 2003), 1:283.
2. Walter Brueggemann, *Reverberations of Faith: A Theological Handbook of Old Testament Themes* (Louisville, TN: Westminster John Knox Press, 2002), 232
3. Ibid., 233
4. Raymond Scheindlin, *The Book of Job* (New York: Norton, 1999), 21.

Chapter Six

THE POWER OF QUESTIONS (Job 6–8)

In the creation story, after God instructs Adam and Eve on what not to do, the serpent asks the first question in the Bible: "Did God really say you must not eat the fruit from any of the trees in the garden?" (Genesis 3:1, NLT). But in the cool of the evening, God comes to Adam and Eve with the next questions: "Where are you?" . . . "Who told you that you were naked?" . . . "Have you eaten from the tree whose fruit I commanded you not to eat?" (3:9, 11, NLT). Then the Lord God asks the woman, "What have you done?" (3:13, NLT). The act of asking questions is as old as humanity. The urge to ask questions is an inborn, God-given human trait.

In our information age, we sometimes neglect to consider the power of questions in our learning and growth processes. We rush to provide information rather than offer questions. Job and God raise more than two hundred questions in the Book of Job. Learning demands questions. Growth requires answers. Perhaps many relationships fail because of fear and failure to ask sufficient questions. Whether between friends, spouses, or even with God, we might imagine what it is like to build or nurture a relationship without a few pertinent questions. Unfortunately, we are not prepared to hear some answers in our relationships. The unwillingness to ask eventually can become one's nemesis.

We cannot understand the depth and scope of this biblical book without wrestling with the questions Job raised to those around him and to God as he faithfully offered sacrifices. Job posed questions in all his relationships. For example, he responds to Zophar in Job 21:4 with the question, "Is my complaint directed to a human being? Why should I not be impatient?" When responding to his wife regarding their shared struggle and dilemma, he asks, "Should we accept only good things from the hand of God and never anything bad?" (2:10, NLT). Job is not only choosing to move toward God with questions gushing from the ocean of pain and passion in his soul, but he is crafting such questions out of his need to know and to grow in his increasing ability to trust God. These questions help shape Job's relationship with God even as they are difficult questions.

Enquiring Minds

In the 1980s, the tabloid *The National Enquirer* chose the slogan, "Enquiring minds want to know," which effectively became their brand. This slogan quickly transformed into a new hip saying that caught on widely and was seen in TV ads.[1] As the largest-selling supermarket tabloid in the US, the motto eventually took on a life of its own. They eventually modified the phrase by changing from the British spelling of the word to the US spelling, resulting in "Inquiring minds want to know" as a variant of the expression appearing throughout popular culture.

Job has quite an inquiring mind, as evidenced by his far more profound questions than any tabloid could raise. In his relentless interrogation of God, Job seeks answers from God to assuage the turmoil in his own mind and the dilemma in his soul. He often declares, "If only I knew where to find him; if only I could go to his dwelling!" (23:3). Job's proliferation of questions eventually leads him out of the darkness enveloping his life, moving him toward the light he seeks in God's presence. Job's anguished, inquisitive searches initially produce no results. Even with his inquiring mind and persistent soul, Job cannot find the God he thought he knew:

> But if I go to the east, he is not there;
> if I go to the west, I do not find him.
> When he is at work in the north, I do not see him;
> when he turns to the south, I catch no glimpse of him.
> But he knows the way that I take;
> when he has tested me, I will come forth as gold.
>
> —23:8-10

Because Job realizes that God knows "the way that [he takes]" (23:10), Job finally sees a glimmer of hope on the horizon. He quickly recognizes that God knows right where he is no matter what he faces. Job is convinced that God knows him and that he knows God. However, he seems more secure in the latter than in the former. Such assurance pulsates through his speeches, which are rife with questions hurled at God about his human plight. The fact becomes quite clear in how he wrestles with God via his verbalized frustration and anxious questions. Job senses that God does not grasp the urgent need to change Job's situation and end this human misery. As readers of this book, we know that at the end of God's test of Job, Job is sure that his relationship with God will be valued and proven as pure as the world's most precious metal: gold!

Gaining Comfort with Questions

Many believers may hesitate to raise questions with God, thinking that doing so could indicate a lack of faith. However, questions reflect the pursuit of a deeper relationship that ensures, nurtures, and supports a mature faith. The Book of Job confirms that our faith develops deeply along the continuum of our personal questions.

Some faith traditions encourage questions as part of their discipleship and learning processes, even as far as inclusion in ceremonies. For example, the Passover seder begins, "Why is this night different from all other nights?" and continues with three additional questions about the traditions. The practice of asking questions differs between cultures. For example, Judaic traditions emphasize asking questions in a group experience with God. In American Christianity, questions tend to be of an independent, individual nature when establishing a relationship with God.[2] When Jesus declared, "You should not be surprised at my saying, 'You must be born again'" (John 3:7), he was not speaking to the nation of Israel but to the individuals he called to follow him. Therefore, belief in him did not require a Jewish heritage (consider the value many place on a *personal* relationship with God).

At the very root of a Jewish collective identity is how they were freed from Egypt: collectively; how they received God's covenant: collectively; and how they were led into the Promised Land: collectively. The concept of a collective faith is confirmed in biblical texts such as, "Then [God] said, "I am the God of your father, the God of Abraham, the God of Isaac and the God of Jacob . . ." and "So now, go. I am sending you to Pharaoh to bring my people the Israelites out of Egypt" (Exodus 3:6, 10). These two verses among many other Hebrew texts confirm the covenant God made with the Hebrew nation he formed as a people and not covenants with faithful individuals. Additionally, God already confirmed them as the only group in this covenant when God said, "I will make you into a great nation, and I will bless you; I will make your name great, and you will be a blessing. I will bless those who bless you, and whoever curses you I will curse; and all peoples on earth will be blessed through you" (Genesis 12:2-3).

God did not scatter them; rather, he gathered them into one group for his namesake and his glory, in stark contrast to the Christians who were ordered as individual believers to scatter, if you will, into all the world as individual people of faith, not as a collected national group: "Therefore go and make disciples of all nations, baptizing them in the name of the Father and of the Son and of the Holy Spirit, and teaching them to obey everything I have commanded you. And surely I am with you always, to the very end of the age" (Matthew 28:19-20).

Jesus also said, "My Father's house has many rooms; if that were not so, would I have told you that I am going there to prepare a place for you?" (John 14:2). Not just one room for all, but many rooms with individuals in mind.

Jonathan Udren, as part of the Chabad-Lubavitch Hasidic Jews, pictures the Torah not just as one complete unit but also, more fundamentally, as six hundred thousand individual parts. He says that "the body has its collective form, which is the entity of the Nation as a whole. . . . Just before the Nation received the Torah at Mt. Sinai, we see a vivid description of Israel as a healthy body with the sum of its parts working in perfect harmony. . . . Perhaps the most famous Torah commentator, Rabbi Shlomo Yitzchaki, known as Rashi, [declares that] 'Israel at that point in the journey was "as one being, with one heart."'" According to Udren, they were "in the process making a vessel through which to receive the gift of the Torah."[3]

The Christian religion seems far more individualized: freed from sin upon individual confession, a personal covenant with God through Jesus Christ, and a promised place with God in eternity: individualized. A historic spiritual song confirms this sentiment and understanding as voiced in one's passionate plea:

> Not my brother, not my sister, but it's me O Lord,
> Standin' in the need of prayer. . . .
> Not the preacher, not the deacon, but it's me, O Lord,
> Standin' in the need of prayer. . . .
> Not my father, not my mother, but it's me, O Lord,
> Standin' in the need of prayer.[4]

The Book of Job begins with awareness of the collective, revealing Job's habit of offering sacrifices to God—not just for himself, but for each of his children as well. Yet the book concludes with a focus on Job's individual quest to know God personally. God requires Job to make peace with those who originally came to comfort him and keep him within their religious fold. Job 42:10 declares, "After Job had prayed for his friends, the LORD restored his fortunes and gave him twice as much as he had before" (42:10). Job's personal journey, from the collective nature of religious practice to a personal relationship with God, returns to a focus on the collective. Reflecting on the resolution, Emil G. Kraeling penned, "Thus, the book of Job enters that exalted sphere where the religious experience looms so large that nothing else matters."[5]

Over our lifetimes, how often do we follow a similar spiritual journey? Sometimes we need the ritual and reassurance of our faith communities, and at other times we need time to work out our personal relationship with God. Don't we really need both collective and individual experiences for spiritual growth and support, just as Job did?

My Spiritual Growth through Questions

I was raised in a Christian home and attended church from the time I was a baby in arms. By the age of four, I was an active believer, and I committed my life to Jesus Christ at the age of seven. As a young woman, I began to raise some questions about God, as so many others do. When I asked them aloud, Dad sought to correct me because he believed I shouldn't question God. I convinced him that I was not questioning God's existence or reality. Like Job's questions, my questions were deeper. I had questions about the very presence of God at the point of my need. As a youngster, I was passionately seeking to fathom what God was doing in my life and to grasp where God was when I needed God the most. Naturally, a discussion ensued. I ended it with the pronouncement that if God was not big enough to answer my questions, then God was not big enough to be my God! Like Job, I, too, found out that God could handle any questions I could lob at him. And I realized, as Job did, that God knew right where I was in any devastating moment or catastrophic situation.

In a miraculous way, the questions I wrestled with grew my faith in ways that just reading through Scriptures or memorizing favorite texts had not and could not do. Sunday school teachers, Christian leaders, and preachers usually emphasize the study of God's Word as the way to increase our faith. These faith-shaping activities are undoubtedly critically important, but perhaps they generate more knowledge than faith, and the two are not always the same. Most believers can repeat carefully selected biblical texts, but the condition of our world is sufficient evidence that some folks do not actually know how to apply what they quote. It is unclear if they have even taken God's Word to heart! Faith development necessitates a wrestling match with God—not only in the good times but, most importantly, in moments when life is diminished, demeaned, diverted, or destroyed.

No human can escape the experience of wondering, *Where is God?* We all have likely been in situations where we asked that question out loud or in the secret compartments of our hearts. But that question can reroute us back to the path of feeling God's presence and seeing signs of God's power to do great things in our lives.

Trusting God through Doubt

Some years ago, I was in a Barnes & Noble bookstore perusing the religious section and happened upon a book titled *Godwrestling—Round Two: Ancient Wisdom, Future Paths* by Rabbi Arthur O. Waskow.[6] I started laughing so hard that folks peered around the book aisles, wondering what was going on. The question that prompted my laughter and piqued my interest was, who won round one? Of course, I knew God did, but it felt so comical at the moment because I was curious why the author started with round two. The book describes many Old Testament heroes who wrestled with God in some way, and Job would be in that number. My question in the bookstore immediately reminded me of the Book of Job, knowing he had already lost round one in the prologue. But then God opens round two to deny victory to Satan and bless the rest of the world. God eventually replies to Job's queries in speeches that Rabbi Victor E. Reichert characterizes as "one spectacular irrelevance to the plot of the book." Why so? Because God does not provide Job with a single direct answer to Job's plethora of questions. Instead, God demands that Job gird up and answer his questions. Inherent in God's questions are the answers Job needs and seeks.

Doubts can assail and diminish faith if not handled with focus and intention. Some folks cannot work through those doubts to a point of faith, which takes a toll on their commitment to God. Their faith might be too nascent and immature to power through their doubts. Plus, the nature of the questions or doubts means that some questions might be more religious or academic than spiritual. Some questions are raised to meet an immediate need rather than to develop a robust faith. When we experience evil, we can be assailed by doubts. As the French philosopher Paul Ricoeur wrote, "This image of *homo cum deo* implies the highest conceivable freedom, the freedom to step into the very fabric of the universe, a new formula for man's collaboration with the creative process and the only one to protect man from the terror of existence."[8]

Questions like the ones Job raised about his continued existence may seem like they have no logical answers. Job doesn't find suitable solutions to his problems as he seeks, but that doesn't matter. When we suffer, like Job, we will eventually see God, which is enough. In God, we will find our answers. The Book of Job reflects what St. John of the Cross referred to as "the dark night of the soul,"[9] suggesting that to trust God in the light is easy, but trusting God in the dark requires faith. Enduring darkness is merely preparation. In the next section, we'll examine specific questions shaping Job's path. How might these questions relate to our own experiences as people of faith who have moments of doubt?

Wayfinding through Difficult Questions

We might think of some historical figures such as Martin Luther, Immanuel Kant, Alfred Tennyson, Carl Jung, Martin Buber, and Robert Frost as having Job-like experiences. We may see evidence of similar stories through their work. We might also think of times in our own lives that have felt similarly trying, and we question the meaning or purpose of our own existence. Full of regret and recrimination, Job's first question for God was, "Why did I not perish at birth, and die as I came from the womb?" (3:11).

Because of his profound suffering and multiple losses, Job simply wishes he was never born. Experiencing such anguish, Job would prefer, in that moment, that he was stillborn to preclude the travesty of the life he is experiencing. Such depth of pain and sorrow is not beyond our human imagination. Most of us have been there. Reports of traumatic experiences fill our newspapers, cable news, and social media pages every day. And in the same chapter, Job's agony deepens. He asks, "Why is light given to those in misery?" (3:20). "Why is life given to a man whose way is hidden, whom God has hedged in?" (3:23).

After Eliphaz chimes in, Job fires a barrage of eighteen questions that are rife with anger, disappointment, and delusion, including these: "If misery could be weighed, if you could pile the whole bitter load on the scales, it would be heavier than all the sand of the sea! Is it any wonder that I'm screaming like a caged cat?" (6:2-3, MSG), and "Is tasteless food eaten without salt?" (6:6). When life has been so ravaged, it has lost its flavor. We see this with people who are in despair. Grief leaves us feeling unable to eat or enjoy things we love. Grief oscillates and cycles through stages, including anger. Questions like these are certain to arrive in moments of personal trial.

Job also asks, "What strength do I have, that I should still hope? What prospects, that I should be patient?" (6:11). Job's words recognize that even in our weakest hour, to have a bit of meager hope requires some level of spiritual strength. He continues, "Do I have the strength of stone? Is my flesh bronze?" (6:12). "Do you mean to correct what I say, and treat my desperate words as wind?" (6:26). "Is there any wickedness on my lips? Can my mouth not discern malice?" (6:30). "What is mankind that you make so much of them?" (7:17). Can you feel these questions intensifying? Job was not only rebutting his friends, but his anger toward God was growing stronger!

This one statement may convince us of Job's frustration: "Will you not look away from me for a while, let me alone until I swallow my spittle?" (Job 7:19, NRSV). This is one of Job's most poignant questions, and it seriously conveys his impatience with God. Job *needed* an immediate answer. He wrestled with God and attempted to wring out of this experience some new understanding about his life, if not also about his God and the ensuing relationship that requires the bond of faith.

Job was convinced of his divine source, but he was uncertain whether God was still with him, given the depth of his pain and suffering. Job initially wrestled with his mortality, as most of us would do. He was convinced of his powerlessness before the Almighty, who could easily turn him to dust again: "Can mere mortals prove their innocence before God?" (9:2). "Who could say to him, 'What are you doing?'" (9:12). "You know that I am not guilty and that no one can rescue me from your hand[.] Your hands shaped me and made me. Will you now turn and destroy me? Remember that you molded me like clay. Will you now turn me to dust again?" (10:7-9). "Why then did you bring me out of the womb?" (10:18).

Job moves from the reality of his flesh and the reality that God rules over all flesh, including the animal kingdom, into a very different self-understanding. Job realizes that it was not his flesh that God was most concerned about but his soul—the very breath that God blew into Adam as found in Genesis 2:7 when "man became a living soul" (KJV).

In his quest for a better relationship, Job seeks the hidden God with whom he wants to be friends! No longer was God just the caretaker and "watcher of men" (7:20b, NKJV) as in Job's earlier perception of God. Now he asked, "Why do you hide your face and consider me your enemy? For you write down bitter things against me and make me reap the sins of my youth" (13:24, 26). "Who can bring what is pure from the impure? No one!" (14:4). Job wants to see God's face, to know God more personally, and not be regarded as one whom God rejects from the Divine presence. So, he then reaches into eternity—still longing to know this God—seeking a sliver of hope that might help him perceive that there will be something after his flesh becomes dirt again. In another significant step on his journey beyond mere religion and toward a life-sustaining faith, Job beseeches God, "Oh that you would hide me in Sheol, that you would conceal me until your wrath is past, that you would appoint me a set time, and remember me! If mortals die, will they live again? All the days of my service I would wait until my release should come" (14:13-14, NRSV).

Job makes it clear that although he is sparring with his friends Bildad, Eliphaz, and Zophar, he knows quite well that his complaint is far weightier than a mere discussion with other earthlings who could wield little if any power over him. He perceives God's failure to answer as anger, which God does not manifest when God finally arrives. Job still operates transactionally—that is, there should be some realized benefit (if not guaranteed outcome) as a result of worshipping and praying to God. His transactional theology forces him to raise these subsequent questions. Of course, no benefit on demand exists in the divine-human relationship, but Job doesn't realize it yet. He is only on the way. "What is the Almighty, that we should serve him? And what profit do we get if we pray to him?" (21:15, NRSV).

Then to Zophar, Job spews out something that today might sound like, "How, then, can you confront me with nonsense?" Job's frustration with his friends amps up, especially as he recalls the good he has done for so many others. He recalls the justice he has meted out in the lives of both his male and female servants, then raises the question, "If I have dismissed the case of my male or female servants when they made a complaint against me, what could I do when God stands up to judge?" (31:13-14, HCSB).

Job does not have to wait long for an answer. God is ready to address every question Job raises. God also brings the divine perspective to their relationship in that God has a few questions for Job. God's questions are by no means direct answers for Job. On the contrary, they put all of Job's questions into their proper perspective of what a divine-human relationship is and must be! Such questions become a serious reckoning with God's omnipotence. Job's only response is to clasp his hand over his mouth and say nothing more except that he can finally *see* God for himself after only "hearing about" God all these years (42:5).

What answers does God share with us through questions in our lives? What are some ways we clearly see God's presence after moments of doubt? As we continue in this chapter, I invite you to think about how we work through our questions in our hope of seeing God more clearly.

Working through Your Own Questions

When reckoning with your doubts, thoughts, or troubles, do not ignore any of the questions that arise in your mind, prick your soul, or seem to assault your very being. Raise them until someone hears you—especially when that someone just might eventually be God, coming to restore the peace and contentment for which your soul longs. Our questions lead to our fulfillment of God's purpose for us. After sensing a call to ministry in 1971, it took me six years of raising questions before I was convinced. The church said no. The Baptist denomination said no. Even the seminary I attended said no. But I kept questing for further confirmation from God with unceasing questions. One pastor asked me to leave his church when, as a worship leader, this statement leaped from my spirit as we celebrated Women's Day: "Though God made woman second in time, that didn't mean that made her second best." My working through the questions to heed God's call brought me to where I am today after serving as a minister, educator, author, preacher, church consultant, and seminary professor.

Differences in gender, calling, race, nationality, educational level, or social standing should not diminish anybody's worth or opportunity, as God values and loves us all equally as God's children. But often, getting to that assuredness and confidence takes raising questions to society, self, and God. The Book of Job confirmed that reality for me. Our daily lives are shaped by questions that we take for granted: "What's for dinner?" "Where is . . . ?" "How do I do . . . ?" "Will you go with me?" and so on. Questions take us where we want to go or propel us toward what we want or need to become. Without the profusion of questions from my head and heart, I would have had a career in the banking world instead of ministry on four continents and in many of the United States. Job sets a high standard for us all.

Below, I invite you to consider the role of questions in shaping your life and relationship with God. In the next chapter, we will witness how Job leverages the power of his conversation with God to find peace amid suffering.

Questions for Reflection and/or Response

1. Reflect on some of the ways questions help us learn. What are some ways the act of asking questions has

changed the trajectory of your day? Your plans? Your life?

2. What questions might you ask to help you "see" God or perceive God more greatly?
3. Every major biblical person wrestled with God in or because of their circumstances. How or over what have you wrestled with God through the power or urgency of your questions?
4. When you feel as if you've searched for God east, west, north, and south as Job did, where do you find consolation? What sustained your soul through times when you wondered where God was in your life?
5. Why are Christians sometimes uncomfortable with asking God questions?
6. Identify two Scriptures you depend on when you are stressed and are not hearing or finding God.

Notes

1. James Kiso, "Enquiring Minds Want to Know," AUE, accessed June 3, 2023, https://www.alt-usage-english.org/excerpts/fxenquir.html.
2. Walter Brueggemann, *Reverberations of Faith: A Theological Handbook of Old Testament Themes* (Louisville, KY: Westminster John Knox Press, 2002), 232.
3. Jonathan Udren, "Individuality and the Collective," Chabad.org, accessed June 3, 2023, https://www.chabad.org/kabbalah/article_cdo/aid/380521/jewish/Individuality-and-the-Collective.htm.
4. "Standing in the Need of Prayer," African American spiritual, hymnary.org, public domain.
5. Emil G. Kraeling, "A Theodicy—and More," in Nahum N. Glatzer's, *The Dimensions of Job: A Study and Selected Readings* (New York: Schocken, 1987), 213.
6. Arthur O. Waskow, *Godwrestling—Round Two: Ancient Wisdom, Future Paths* (Woodstock, VT: Jewish Lights, 1996).
7. Victor E. Reichert, *Job* (Hindhead, Surrey, UK: Soncino, 1946), 12.
8. Paul Ricoeur, *The Symbolism of Evil* (Boston: Beacon, 1967), 361.
9. John of the Cross, "The Dark Night: Stanzas of the Soul by St. John of the Cross," CatholicLink, accessed June 3, 2023, https://catholic-link.org/quotes/the-dark-night-stanzas-of-the-soul-st-john-of-the-cross-poem/.

Chapter Seven

FROM "WHY ME?" TO "WHY NOT ME?" (Job 23–24, 29, 31)

> I was eyes to the blind
> and feet to the lame.
> I was a father to the needy,
> and I championed the cause of the stranger.
> I broke the fangs of the unrighteous
> and made them drop their prey from their teeth.
>
> —Job 29:15-17 (NRSV)

Likely all of us have said or thought, "Why me?" Probably fewer of us have reached the point of asking, "Why not me?" Think about the last time you asked, "Why me?" How did you feel about asking God, or anyone, why you had to suffer? Feeling powerless, alone, or isolated can easily trigger a sense of victimhood. From my observations and experiences, the sequence of events preceding something traumatic can predispose us to see ourselves as victims. Job is certainly no exception.

As Job reflects on his life in the text above, we learn that he was quite involved in serving the needs of many folks in his community. Before he asks in chapter 24 why the wicked are not punished, Job voices a long list of evils in chapter 23.

He sees evil folks perpetuating the suffering of others—his family included—which plants the seeds for seeing himself as a victim. Before his current traumas, he had prior traumas, such as evil folks stealing his land and livestock. Job's new troubles resurrected latent feelings, not only because he was aware of present evils beyond his family enclave but because of what he had seen and felt at the hands of those who meant him evil. He not only mentions murderers, adulterers, and thieves, but he says that "wicked people rebel against the light. They refuse to acknowledge its ways or stay in its paths" (24:13, NLT).

We see Job's growth in his reflections about his earlier benevolence toward the community in addition to the information he gives about his exemplary lifestyle. His memory supports his self-perception of goodness and affirms he committed no sin that could have earned him such suffering. On one hand, he sought to justify himself. On the other hand, he simply reported the quality of life he lived: affliction without cause.

As "eyes for the blind" (29:15a), Job could see what was needed—or even what others refused to see—within the community long before others could discern it. Similarly, Job did not fear walking where others dared not trod, potentially in their civic duties, cries for justice, or even political needs. Then "I searched out (stood up for) the cause of him whom I did not know" (29:16, ESV). Such words become reminiscent of several historical leaders whose lives mattered because other people's lives mattered to them. For example, President Lyndon Baines Johnson, amid the 1960s Civil Rights struggle, signed the Voting Rights Act into law to ensure that every American had access to the ballot box.[1] In more recent years, President Barack Obama worked feverishly to pass what was derisively called "ObamaCare." Then, Republican Senator John McCain of Arizona voted down the Republican effort that would have gutted the bill. The bill was saved, giving better healthcare to millions.[2] Our world needs leaders like

Job. We may think of local leaders in our own communities like this, but two major examples who fit this description on a historic scale are Mahatma Gandhi and Martin Luther King Jr.

Twentieth-Century Jobs

If you were reading the story of Job without the context of studying the Bible, you might envision such renowned leaders and historical giants as Mohandas Karamchand Gandhi (known as Mahatma Gandhi) or the Reverend Dr. Martin Luther King Jr. These leaders led struggles for justice and freedom within their lifetimes, and their actions continue to resonate in ours. Their private and public suffering worked to catalyze their greater leadership. Job's leadership occurred before his suffering, but his deep reflection on it helped transform the rest of his life.

I have understood Job as the Martin Luther King Jr. of the Old Testament for years. For this reason, I have used this text as the basis for such annual celebrations of King's life. Others associate King with the Amos 5:24 text, "Let justice run down like water, and righteousness like a mighty stream" (King's paraphrase). This verse was the basis of King's address to the first Montgomery Improvement Association (MIA) mass meeting at the Holt Street Baptist Church in Montgomery, Alabama, on December 5, 1955. This biblical text greatly defined his ministry and his efforts toward civil justice in memorable ways. However, I believe that this text in Job provides a glimpse into the personal motivations that drove King's actions to improve our country and world.

Job's story defines the life and work of Mahatma Gandhi as well. It is said that Christian missionaries sought to convert the Mahatma on his arrival in South Africa. Having failed, they may have whetted his appetite a bit for religious studies. One famous conclusion that he eventually reached and declared was, "Jesus Christ, *yes*! Christianity?

No!"[3] And for him, there was no equivocation. The Mahatma easily discerned the difference between religious practices and the purity of faith. With a voracious mind and a deeply benevolent spirit, this declaration is evidence that he had delved deeply into studying Christianity and other major religions. However, nothing nourished his soul like the religion of his birth—Hinduism. Whether the Mahatma ever read Job or allowed its powerful vision of fighting for justice to inform or support his efforts toward justice and reconciliation is anyone's guess, but his life fully reflects this biblical model nestled within the Hebrew scriptures. Gandhi reckoned that true religion was more a matter of the heart than of the intellect and that genuine beliefs were those that were literally lived. Gandhi believed the real test of anyone's spiritual progress was how people could translate their beliefs into work-a-day life. The book that became Gandhi's bond with Hinduism, as well as the greatest influence on him, was the *Bhagavad Gita*.[4]

These two global warriors for justice share an amazing connection. In 1987, I was invited by Sri Rajmohan Gandhi, a grandson of the Mahatma, to come to India and share in events celebrating the lives of both the Mahatma and Dr. King. This assembled international group participated in what he called a *yatra*, a Sanskrit word that suggests a pilgrimage to a holy site—a reflective journey in which participants can draw greater meaning and purpose into life. And that it did! The younger Gandhi planned the yatra for October of that year to celebrate the Mahatma's birthday and to retrace his grandfather's Salt March, which ended at Dandi Beach and ultimately freed India from British rule.[5] The journey served as an orientation to and reflective journey of the essence and power of *satyagraha*. From Sanskrit, the roots of this word (1) *satya* means "truth, essence," and (2) *agraha* means "insistence." *Satyagraha* can be loosely translated as "insistence on truth" or "holding on to truth." These participants were already serving their communities in personal and organized efforts of reconciliation in various cities in America and other countries as well.

Various native Indian delegations joined us along the way, but I recall that well over one hundred participants engaged in this journey together from quite a variety of countries, representing about twelve different world religions. This ecumenical experience was important to me because I had been asked to prepare four messages to share during the yatra beginning at Dandi Beach, at various points along the way, and during the celebration. This text from Job was one. Though the yatra identified no specific religious adherence, such an effort left no doubt that each participant's faith laid some requirements on them to foster peace in our world. The yatra left no doubt that a serious religious commitment and challenge were at its very root: to live what we believe.

Participants celebrated this connection as we retraced the famous Salt March from Dandi Beach to Ahmedabad, Gujarat. The original march took twenty-five days and covered 240 miles. The legacy of peaceful protest that Job defined for himself in this text (29:15-17) continued from Gandhi to King, who declared in a recorded interview in India,

> Since being in India, I am more convinced than ever before that the method of nonviolent resistance is the most potent weapon available to oppressed people in their struggle for justice and human dignity.[5]

Gandhi, a British-trained lawyer who lived in South Africa, knew the Gospels and probably had a deep understanding of the Old Testament. He may have thought of Job's suffering as Gandhi himself suffered. King, steeped in the Bible, would have known about Job and understood suffering in many ways. More importantly for us, we might ask whether Job's message is as relevant to our society and communities today. Job was fully "woke" to the needs of his community and, to the best of his ability, allowed no need to go unmet.

But today, we have political leaders fighting against the "wokeness" they disdain and seeking instead to return to their caves of intentional social blindness, academic contempt, and racial ignorance! Might we yet be *eyes for the blind* for those who still refuse to see the worth and dignity of every human being regardless of color or ethnicity? Might we become *feet for the lame* to march for those who refuse to walk in peaceful protests for the cause of justice and freedom? Might we *stand up for the cause of those whom we do not know* simply because we know their value as human beings, as children of God, and as citizens within our democracy?

Some people report a connection between the suffering and injustices they see or experience with finding their purpose. The resulting sacrifice of their lives, or the prevailing work that grew from their experiences, ultimately defines their life's work. For Job, that suffering included painful sores and the loss of family, fame, and fortune. Reflecting on his life before the tragedies was a defining moment for Job. As we continue examining Job's story, we will witness a mindset transformation, in which Job moves from asking "Why me?" in response to his suffering to "Why not me?"

Differences in Mindset

A *why me?* mindset can be psychologically isolating, as it can be like placing ourselves outside of the human family. All humans endure suffering at some point in their lives. A *why not me?* mindset, such as Job's rhetoric eventually suggests, recognizes that no person is beyond the possibility of suffering. As humans, we lack the wisdom to solve the mystery of suffering; we can only stand in reverence or fear of God. Whether Job had an elitist spirit or sense of exceptionalism that flowed from his religion or from his honored position within the community is impossible to know. Job had lived a good, long life, becoming not only prosperous but respected, honored, and even celebrated at the gate of the city. He said,

When I went to the gate of the city
and took my seat in the public square,
the young men saw me and stepped aside
and the old men rose to their feet;
the chief men refrained from speaking
and covered their mouths with their hands;
the voices of the nobles were hushed,
and their tongues stuck to the roof of their mouths.
Whoever heard me spoke well of me,
and those who saw me commended me,
because I rescued the poor who cried for help,
and the fatherless who had none to assist them.
The one who was dying blessed me;
I made the widow's heart sing.
I put on righteousness as my clothing;
justice was my robe and my turban.

—29:7-14

But such a lofty status was then fully negated or reversed by the sores that covered his body and the loss of everything that connected him to his community. Job's friends arrived and were immediately rendered speechless because of the heinous change in Job's appearance. And because of that appearance, Job could no longer sit at the city gate to engage with friends and those passing by. When calamities strike, we not only experience internal pain but a pulling away from those most familiar to us. How do you react in times of personal tragedies such as these? Do your pride and self-esteem take a beating? Are you more prone to isolate yourself at a time when you just might need folks the most?

Suffering, of course, can be either destructive or redemptive. The Job story forces us to wonder whether life's traumas and catastrophes have a divine purpose in our lives. But the sufferer must securely emerge from the depths of self-pity borne by asking, "Why me?" To emerge from suffering, we must make the emotional and spiritual journey toward a more confident stance of "Why not me?" thus refusing to see ourselves as outliers to the human experience. With that question, we reignite our mental, emotional, and spiritual capacities to recover from trauma and rejoin the human family.

We will further explore Job's journey that moved beyond his earlier religious commitment (reflected in his sacrificial acts) toward a more personalized faith. His own words, "Now my eyes have seen you" (42:5)—the God he could not find earlier—allowed him to escape his self-pity. This statement clearly suggests a deeper, more spiritually viable relationship. Job was now progressing from a state of physical and spiritual weakness to a more psychologically confident state. And I suggest that, emotionally and spiritually, he also moved from the isolation of *why me?* to a more inclusive *why not me*? worldview. So how did Job make this journey?

Job's Transformational Journey

We understand from the outset of the Book of Job that he was a righteous man who believed in God and sought to do His work. In Job 29, he recalled his life before Satan's torment. For example, verses 1-6 (NRSV) read:

> Job again took up his discourse and said:
> "Oh, that I were as in the months of old,
> as in the days when God watched over me;
> when his lamp shone over my head,
> and by his light I walked through darkness;
> when I was in my prime,
> when the friendship of God was upon my tent;
> when the Almighty was still with me,
> when my children were around me;
> when my steps were washed with milk,
> and the rock poured out for me streams of oil!"

Job's religious commitment propelled him into action for the cause of justice and the beneficial care of others: "I was a father to the needy, and I championed the cause of the stranger. I broke the fangs of the unrighteous, and made them drop their prey from their teeth" (29:16-17).

Job was seen as a wise, wealthy, and worthy man. I am not suggesting he had sinless perfection, but rather that he was "blameless and upright" as God declared in 1:8. The prologue asserts that Job was the singular specimen among humanity who best represented God's purposes for humans here on earth. And Satan wanted to distort that.

I perceive that in Job's journey through religion toward a personalized faith, his friends pushed him to come to grips with four valid questions that we must move through (and even beyond) in our arduous trek from mere religiosity toward faith:

1. Who am I in relation to . . . ?
2. What do I know of God?
3. What do I believe about God?
4. What do I do as a consequence of what I know and believe?

This sense of movement in the story is a possible literary device, and these questions project a sense of mystery in Job's friends' theological arguments. Yet we also move toward the crescendo of Job's personal declaration of faith in the God who challenged the width, breadth, and depth of his human power.

These questions are not limited to Job or Job-like experiences; they are threads of the very fabric of our existential angst. They become essential in our search for meaning and purpose. They are simple but profound entities in our movement toward the universe's ultimate power—God. No one speaks after Job but Elihu, who presents himself as a lawyer in a courtroom, before God has his say and gives Job a bit of a comeuppance.

Job concludes his speeches with a profound sense of repentance, uttering sixteen *ifs* that encompass religious infractions or misbehaviors of which he feels he may have been guilty. In chapter 31, a spiritual sense of regret and repentance moves him closer to his declaration of faith, which we find just ten chapters later!

> *If* I have walked with falsehood . . . (31:5)
> *if* my steps have turned from the path . . . (31:7)
> *if* my hands have been defiled . . . (31:7)
> *If* my heart has been enticed by a woman . . . (31:9)
> *If* I have rejected the cause of my male or female slaves . . . (31:13)
> *If* I have denied justice to any of my servants . . . (31:13)
> *If* I have denied the desires of the poor or let the eyes of the widow grow weary . . . (31:16)
> *if* I have seen anyone perishing for lack of clothing, or the needy without garments . . . (31:19)
> *if* I have raised my hand against the fatherless . . . (31:21)
> *If* I have put my trust in gold or said to pure gold, "You are my security" . . . (31:24)
> *if* I have rejoiced over my great wealth . . . (31:25)
> *if* I have regarded the sun in its radiance or the moon moving in splendor . . . (31:26)
> *If* I have rejoiced at my enemy's misfortune or gloated over the trouble that came to him . . . (31:29)
> *if* those of my household have never said, "Who has not been filled with Job's meat?" . . . (31:31)
> *if* I have concealed my sin as people do, by hiding my guilt in my heart . . . (31:33)
> *If* my land cries out against me and all its furrows are wet with tears . . . (31:38)
> *if* I have devoured its yield without payment . . . (31:39)

But first, Job had to hear disdain and rebuke from Elihu, who believed that Job "was righteous in his own eyes." Elihu was "very angry with Job for justifying himself rather than God" (32:1-2). In disbelief, Elihu quotes Job as saying, "I am pure, I have done no wrong; I am clean and free from sin" (32:8-9). He offers no flattering words to Job nor to his other friends to help Job in his quest to find and know God. He even wonders why Job has contended with God. Then in chapter 33, Elihu makes a quick shift toward the perception that there just might be "an angel . . . a mediator, one out of a thousand, sent to tell them how to be upright, and he is gracious to that person and says to God, 'Spare them from going down to the pit'" (33:23-24). Then Elihu presents this as an answer to Job: "That person can pray to God and find favor with him, they will see God's face and shout for joy; he will restore them to full well-being" (33:26). Elihu suggests this experience as the only way Job will see light again and be removed from the darkness that has engulfed his life.

Elihu was on to something, asserting in his four speeches that Job was not being entirely truthful about his lack of sinning. He seems to have perceived Job as making himself the exception to the rest of humanity as he continuously cries, "Why me?" That's the realm of isolation and darkness, because what God does, God does for all of humanity—not just for a select few, no matter how good they profess to live. In his first speech, Elihu declared, "God does all these things to a person—twice, even three times—to turn them back from the pit, that the light of life may shine on them" (33:29-30). Darkness was beyond the land of the living, he seemed to assert, because it was isolated from the rest of humanity.

Perhaps more than either of the previous speakers, Elihu attempts to beckon Job back into a sense of inclusion within humanity. Elihu's questions thus helped to move Job's spirit from isolation to inclusion, from "Why me?" to "Why not me?" That is a life lesson for us all, because in our worst of times, we psychologically and spiritually tend to isolate ourselves from the rest of humanity, while claiming a level of righteousness that we believe exempts us from deserving such catastrophes as others experience.

Elihu drills down further on that point about Job in his second speech, when he again alludes to Job's sense of exceptionalism. He calls Job out for feeling beyond the ordinary before God, because in his suffering, Job wonders, *What's the use?* This isolating thought pushed Job further, to feel exceptional among other humans. Elihu asked, "Is there anyone like Job, who drinks scorn like water? . . . For he says, 'There is no profit in trying to please God'" (34:6-9). And "Should God then reward you on your terms, when you refuse to repent?" (34:33). Elihu's third speech suggests Job has a sense of a transactional relationship with God, which undermines Job's cries for a healthier relationship with God: "You say, 'I am right, not God.' Yet you ask him, 'What profit is it to me, and what do I gain by not sinning?'" (35:2). Does such a question not sound all too familiar to us once we are in the throes of our hurts and sorrows after having faithfully served God?

Just before Elihu's proclamations, Job had sunk to the lowest of the low when he identified folks who were not his equal on any level, such as young thugs, inexperienced pups, worse than dogs, homeless ragamuffins, outcasts from the community, a gang of beggars, and no-names.

"They violate my broken body, trample through the rubble of my ruined life. . . . My dignity [is] in shreds" (30:15, MSG).

"What did I do to deserve this?" (30:24, MSG).

"I looked for light but darkness fell" (30:27, MSG).

"Didn't the same God who made me, make them? Aren't we all made of the same stuff, equals before God?" (31:15, MSG).

"I'm prepared to account for every move I've ever made—to anyone and everyone, prince or pauper" (31:37, MSG).

Job's friends saw his pain and losses as retributive because they believed he had sinned and deserved all that had come upon him. They lacked the compassion to view it as potentially redemptive, which suffering certainly became in Job's life. Whether we like it or not, the suffering we experience has redemptive power. Job protested their simplistic and rigid responses while professing his innocence. Job experienced the whole gamut of human capacities as he plumbed the depths of his pain, his losses, and consequential suffering. Flailing in his conversations physically, intellectually, psychologically, and spiritually, he descended to the depths of despair with questions that revealed his combativeness not just with his friends but also with God.

Here is the pattern through which Job moved as he sought solace for his suffering and answers to his dilemma even as he launched his "Why me?" primal cry toward a more magnanimous "Why not me?" spirit. Like most humans, our immediate reaction to a personal injury or illness is a "what" question about our physical well-being. Then we try to reason out the catastrophe, scrambling to make some sense of whatever has happened, including, *What did I do to cause it?* or *What could I have done to prevent it?*

Our psyche is the force that allows us to reach more deeply into who we are as unique human individuals to understand our thoughts and personality. We instinctively internalize what has happened to us so that we might connect it with what else matters most to us. Some psychologists make the psyche and soul synonymous, but neither Freud nor Jung did. Psyche (Greek ψυχή), however, means "life," which includes the idea of "spirit" or "soul" as well, or that which animates us as humans.[6] Once Job raises his spiritual questions, he moves beyond himself into a spiritually wider realm that includes others comparable to himself. Job exclaims, "Oh, that I had someone to hear me! I sign now my defense—let the Almighty answer me; let my accuser put his indictment in writing" (31:35).

Like Job's cry, as we call on God to hear us in our circumstances, such a cry is the realization not only that we have no capacity to solve our own dilemma but also that we are not an exception. Though the situation might seem inexplicable, others do have similar experiences that put them into our community of sorrow. We are no longer alone, as our initial "Why me?" serves now to free us from such isolating sentiments and moves us toward faith, eventually taking us into that wider human and spiritual realm of "Why not me?" which reflects the essence of a greater humanity common to us all. It may seem tough and even strange, but oh so necessary, for us to more fully value and validate the human race as a consequence of our encounter with the Divine.

Figure 7.1, on page 101, shows how I diagram that internal movement—how we process the traumatic circumstances that impact our lives and move us toward spiritual faith. As humans, we cannot fully process traumatic events within the scope of our initial reaction. We must process their impact on us within each facet of our humanity. I have plotted such movement on the surface of an ellipse. Movement is clockwise, starting on the right side. This represents dealing with our initial physical reactions to trauma. Like Job, we initially see ourselves as victims—full of despair and self-pity. But with greater religious understanding and maturing spiritually, like Job, we can experience God "in the whirlwind," a theophany in which God's presence becomes clearer to us within our traumatic circumstances. Following the initial shock, we attempt to understand what happened to us.

This paradigm reflects Job's spiritual questing, through a painful dynamic theological tension between him and his friends. Since these dialogues begin on an intense level, it is difficult to sense their incremental rise toward the author's ultimate crescendo, Job's declaration of faith: "I had only heard about you before, but now I have seen you with my own eyes" (42:5, NLT).

By the time we begin psychologically analyzing the problem we've encountered or the trauma we've experienced, we have tapped into our *raison d'être*, considering what has impacted on our lives. By then, we have turned the corner to spiritually reach upward toward some spiritual source for solace. That was the internal journey of Job while sitting on his ash heap:

Physical: "Let the day of my birth be erased" (Job's reaction to his physical illness; 3:3 NLT).

Intellectual: "Why wasn't I born dead? Why didn't I die as I came from the womb?" (3:11, NLT).

Psychological: "Oh, why give light to those in misery, and life to those who are bitter?" (3:20, NLT).

Spiritual: "But he knows the way that I take; when he has tested me, I will come forth as gold" (23:10).

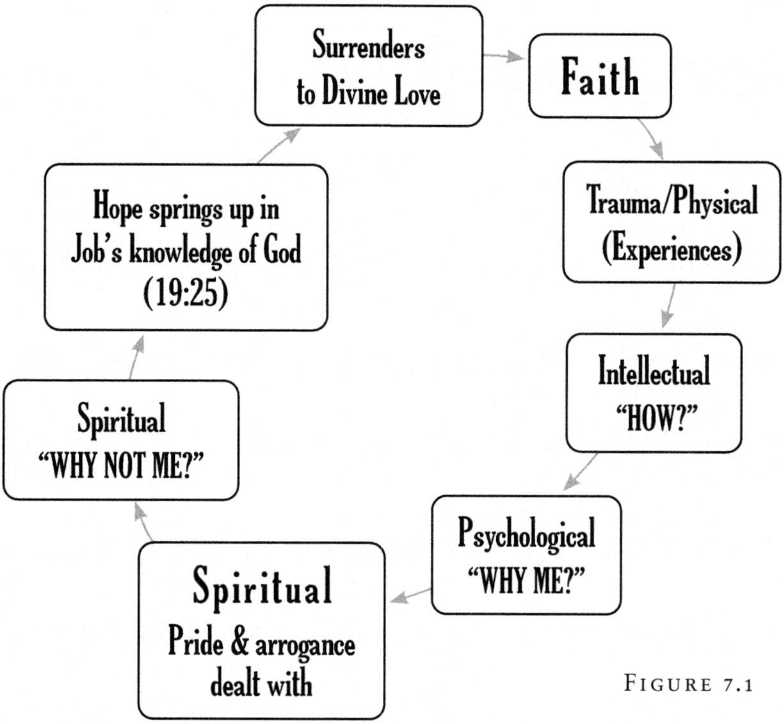

FIGURE 7.1

Job is not finished asking questions nor probing why such things happen to him. Though respectful, if at times intense and demanding, he definitely expects God to answer his questions. God turns the table on Job by demonstrating that some questions are not meant to elicit answers from the hearer but are the answers themselves. God shows that inherent in his questions are the answers Job sought, and if Job listened carefully to God's reverse interrogation, he would have the answers he has so desperately been seeking!

Questions for Reflection and/or Response

1. In what ways does the question "Why me?" serve to isolate you from other people, and why is that not mentally, emotionally, or spiritually healthy?
2. Reflect on Figure 7.1 on page 101, then relate one of your life experiences to it.
3. Does your faith help to extend who you are among other human beings? Explain your answer.
4. Consider how changing the question to "Why not me?" can deepen your sense of belonging to the human family instead of isolating you from it, thus providing a healthier sense of community.
5. Which of God's questions have you answered? Out of more than sixty, here's a sample:

   "Where were you when I . . . ?" (38:4).

   "Does the eagle soar at your command and build its nest on high?" (39:27).

   "Will the one who contends with the Almighty correct him?" (40:2).

   "Would you condemn me to justify yourself?" (40:8).

   "Do you have an arm like God's, and can your voice thunder like his?" (40:9).

Notes

1. Modupe Labode, "John Lewis and Good Trouble," *National Museum of American History*. Washington, D.C., July 18, 2020. https://americanhistory.si.edu/blog/john-lewis.
2. "History of Federal Voting Rights Laws: The Voting Rights Act of 1965," United States Department of Justice. July 28, 2017. Archived from the original on January 6, 2021.
3. Scott Lemieux, "How John McCain saved ObamaCare and proved the haters wrong," *The Week*. July 28, 2017. https://theweek.com/articles/714988/how-john-mccain-saved-obamacare-proved-haters-wrong.
4. Sandhya Mehta, "Gandhiji on Religious Conversion," mkgandhi.org. Accessed June 3, 2023. https://www.mkgandhi.org/ebks/gandhiji-on-religious-conversion.pdf.
5. Evan Andrews, "When Gandhi's Salt March Rattled British Colonial Rule," *History*. August 14, 2023. https://www.history.com/news/gandhi-salt-march-india-british-colonial-rule.
6. "The Psyche in Psychology." *Practical Psychology*, February 21, 2022. https://practicalpie.com/the-psyche/.

Chapter Eight

GOD'S ANSWERS ARE QUESTIONS (Job 38–41)

Having opened in a "courtroom," this biblical saga now moves toward its summit with questions from the Judge, God. God's speeches to Job echo the four themes heard in the interrogatives Job spewed while sitting on his ash heap. First, we see the *Judge vs. the defendant* when God takes up the case that opens the Book of Job. Then, following the *powerful vs. the powerless* theme, Job's fate was decided without his even being present. Job's sorrowfulness, as he is now virtually the most powerless person on earth, seems overwhelming until we realize that most of us end up in the same predicament at some point in our lives. Next, we see the contrast between the *unwise and the wise* when God's wisdom is brought to bear on Job's plight. Last, we see that Job is now quite aware of the contrast between the *created* and *the Creator,* but he is not strongly tuned into the Creator until he surrenders to seeing God rather than merely hearing about him.

Who would have thought that when anticipating answers from God to our questions, we would get questions from God instead? In the Book of Job, we learn that questions are answers, especially when they come from God. Remember, at the beginning of this biblical book, Job was the defendant in absentia and God was the Judge who raised questions with the prosecutor, Satan. Together God and Satan hatched a plan to test Job's religious integrity: would Job curse God or not? Or what would it take to make Job curse God? Satan pushed for a double dose of suffering to prove that Job was not worthy of the abundant blessings he received.

We must not lose sight of the fact that the Creator addresses Job in these many questions that give Job a different perspective of his relationship with God than what Job initially anticipated. God's probing questions remind Job that Job creates nothing worthy of note and has little power over anything that God created. God challenges Job's accusations by taking him on a virtual, interrogative tour of the universe.

Job thought he knew God, but before Job's serial losses and physical suffering, little of God seemed to have been revealed to him. Job served God religiously through a series of rites and sacrifices that he faithfully offered on behalf of himself and his children in case they had sinned. Surprisingly, God does not mention Job's suffering at all. God has not come to commiserate with Job but to ensure that Job will finally know God—not just as Creator but as the authority over the world's moral order with indisputable power over all of creation!

What Job Teaches about Wisdom

We learn from Job that we cannot interpret God through what happens to us; to do so will always skew our view of who God is and how God relates to humanity. However, if we learn to trust God and view our circumstances through what we know of God, then we will not be shaken by what befalls us. Understanding reality in this way ushers in the presence and strength of wisdom in our lives, which is why the Book of Job is designated as one of the wisdom books in the Bible. The only verses in the Book of Job that are not attributed to any speaker are contained in chapter 28, which is devoted to *wisdom*, the wider message of the book.

Raymond Scheindlin asserts that "Job existed before religious doctrine had taken shape when people had no revelation or scriptures to guide them but only experience and age-old wisdom."[1] Brueggemann, however, adds that "wisdom perspectives are as close as the Old Testament comes to scientific thought, for the wisdom teachers give attention to the natural as well as social environment of human life and ponder the regularities of nature."[2] I picture wisdom blossoming like a flower down through the millennia as a result of God's initial instruction to Adam and Eve to "subdue" the earth (Genesis 1:28). The Hebrew word translated as "subdue" in this verse is *kabash*, suggesting "to control, overcome, manage,"[3] and I might add even "to harness" the forces of nature, including community, that humanity will encounter. This automatic exchange for survival's sake is how wisdom blossomed, sustaining life for these millennia. Before religious doctrines were provided or wisdom teachers emerged, God did not fail to guide humanity for their own survival. Our survival is wisdom!

Even without printed Scripture or developed dogma, Job has a relationship with God, as confirmed by both his sacrifices and religious rhetoric. With his daily sacrifices in mind, Job believes that he is faithful to God. But because of his suffering, Job feels not only a sense of alienation from God but separation or distance from God as well. Job knows that he has been faithful to God—doing all that he knew to do to meet the expectations of that relationship—but just as Job's protestations to his friends seek to validate that faithfulness with them, Job's voluminous questions raise doubts about God's faithfulness to him. In 23:2-3 he exclaims, "Even today my complaint is bitter; [God's] hand is heavy in spite of my groaning. If only I knew where to find him; if only I could go to his dwelling!" This phrase seems to confirm the distance and lack of confidence Job now feels defines his relationship with God, undermining any sense of a covenantal relationship. In 16:11, Job says, "God has turned me over to the ungodly and thrown me into the clutches of the wicked." Such a claim suggests a breach in Job's sense of being in covenant with God. His disappointment is palpable; his frustration deepens mainly because he perceives no response from God, as should surely be anticipated within a covenantal relationship. Along with the seeming break in covenant with God, Job simultaneously feels the brokenness in his body. I can hear Job mouthing such sentiments as, "But, God, I thought . . . ," and "But, God, didn't you say . . . ?" and "God, I was taught. . . ." Nothing in Job's awareness in such moments assures him that his covenant with God is still intact.

In our worst of times, we, too, wonder. Don't we? What does it take for you to hold fast to this God-initiated covenant even in your worst of times? How knowledgeable are you about the covenant with God that you entered by faith? Is that covenant only meaningful on Sunday mornings or in your good times? May your faith abound in both the best and worst times of your life as you know—and trust—that God has not and never will forget you. Are you there yet? If not, draw closer and overcome every ill in your life with the faith that God secures for you in the beauty and power of the covenant that he upholds.

I have struggled this past year with a sciatic nerve problem in my right hip and have found it uncomfortable and sometimes downright awkward to bend down to pick up something that fell to the floor. And the worse my condition became, it seemed the more stuff found its way to the floor. That I felt frustrated is an understatement to the nth degree! At times I wanted to utter a foul word or two, but instead, I decided to bless God when something fell to the floor and thank God when I bent to pick it up! That spelled *victory*, which is assured to me, to Job, and to every believer in covenant with a God who has proven to be faithful.

Brueggemann has wisely declared, "The primary and defining issue of [the Old Testament] covenantal relationship is fidelity . . . which is rendered by two terms: 'hesed' and 'emeth'—steadfast love and faithfulness—the core claim of Israel's faith is that God is utterly faithful."[4] This story of Job reflects those sentiments even though it predates the biblical formation of Israel by more than five hundred years, according to many biblical scholars, including Thomas Oden, Tokunboh Adeyemo, Marvin Pope, Anthony Selvaggio, Raymond Scheindlin, Marcus Lefebvre, and Gustavo Gutierrez, whose works have been cited in this book. Brueggemann also says,

> While this notion of suffering is overly simplistic, it also expresses positive theological convictions, affirming that (a) the world is morally coherent and reliable, and (b) that human choices and human conduct are morally significant and contribute decisively to the shape and condition of the future. Such a theologically moral claim is a powerful antidote to the views that human life is meaningless and human conduct is irrelevant.[5]

Job believed in the faithfulness of God though that relationship was pushed to its limits when Job said he looked for God but did not find him (23:8).

The Redemptive Nature of Human Suffering

I am amazed that God never answers Job's questioning of why he suffered such loss, physical pain, and discomfort. Neither does God even intimate to him, "Hey, Job, this is just a test." God chooses not to reveal the backstory that occurred in God's own heavenly courtroom and led to Job's trials. Instead, God raises questions that usher Job into new truths about himself, including the reality that before God, no human is justified. Job's self-justification was Elihu's chief complaint against Job (see 32:2). Finally, Job declares, "No purpose of [God's] can be thwarted" (42:2). And Job then moves from just having heard about God to finally "seeing

God" for himself (42:5), which supports the redemptive nature of human suffering.

Like ours might be, Job's image of God initially seems quite simplistic and transactional. Job's cry for justice is amplified because of the blessings he expects from God and because of his good, benevolent behavior, which his speeches chronicle. Perhaps Job pushes the justice issue so far and so hard that it creates distance between him and God—so much distance that Job says he can't find God in the east, west, north, or south within the universe (23:8). He asks, "Why is life given to a man whose way is hidden, whom God has hedged in?" (3:23).

Job perceives such separation and distance that has not previously defined his relationship with God. Here is a sampling:

> "Therefore I will not keep silent; I will speak out in the anguish of my spirit, I will complain in the bitterness of my soul" (7:11).
>
> "When he passes me, I cannot see him; when he goes by, I cannot perceive him" (9:11).
>
> "If only there were someone to mediate between us, someone to bring us together" (9:33).
>
> "Are not my few days almost over? Turn away from me so I can have a moment's joy" (10:20).
>
> "Only grant me these two things, God, and then I will not hide from you" (13:20).
>
> "Then know that God has wronged me and drawn his net around me. . . . He has blocked my way so I cannot pass; he has shrouded my paths in darkness" (19:6, 8).
>
> "If only I knew where to find him; if only I could go to his dwelling!" (23:3).
>
> "How I long for the months gone by, for the days when God watched over me" (29:2).
>
> "I cry out to you, God, but you do not answer; I stand up, but you merely look at me" (30:20).

God reveals Godself to Job far more deeply than Job had ever experienced, demonstrating majesty, power, and sovereignty through a series of questions that leave Job in awe and bring him to repentance. Through this experience, Job gains a new perspective on God from the mouth of the Creator. This divine perspective is key. Though conversations about Job's sufferings comprise the bulk of the book, God proves what God said at the beginning—that nothing can make Job curse him. I believe God's confidence in Job's eventual grasping of what it means to have faith is the *summum bonum* of this book for us! Significantly, Job learns from his suffering and finally repents.

Job could not have arrived at this point if God had not confronted him with such probing questions that went straight to the heart of the matter. God's profusion of questions, such as, "Where were you Job . . . ?" puts significant and sustained relational distance between Job and the Creator. Job needs to recover, which he does by declaring, "I repent!" The Hebrew word often translated as "repent" is *teshuva*, which means to return. Job's wrestling with God deepens this encounter with God and ultimately restores that blessed relationship.

How powerful are you, Job? Socially? Economically? Professionally? God's questions remind Job that he has no power of his own and no power in comparison to that which God possesses over all creation! The powerful Almighty dresses down a man who has great influence in his community, fueled by his wealth and social generosity, with young men even stepping aside for him at the city gate (29:8). But from God's perspective, this man has no power even to make a crocodile or horse (41:1). Job encounters real power from a Divine source—*creative power*—a source that Job later acknowledges he had only heard about "by the hearing of the ear" (42:5, RSV).

Amazingly, God the Creator asks Job not only *who* he is, but also *what* and *where* he is! God already knows the answers, but the chink in Job's bluster is that God realizes that Job needs to fathom who and what he is relative to God. God puts Job in his place with many remarks and questions that seem sarcastic, which reminds Job of his place within the creation that God yet controls: "Then the LORD answered Job out of the whirlwind: 'Who is this that darkens counsel by words without knowledge? Gird up your loins like a man, I will question you, and you shall declare to me'" (38:1-3, RSV). These verses represent a significant step on a journey toward faith and all that it offers. For we are ones without the level of knowledge the Creator has, regardless of the scientific advances and academic teachings of our time.

The better we probe the depths of any aspect of creation, the less powerful we feel. We revel in the bit of power we do have but stand in awe when facing the evidence of the power we do not have. Consequently, the more we encounter our powerlessness, the greater we reckon with our need for God. Recognizing God's power predisposes us to discern our own limited power as humans as we move along the continuum of faith and the ability to place our trust in God. As Garrett Green says, "The book of Job is informed by and dependent upon the traditions of lament and complaint, but now the matter is presented in a way that is artistically bolder and theologically more daring."[6]

Many of Job's religious assumptions show him to be unwise, not only in his assumptions but in some of the conclusions he draws about the reason for his predicament as well.

Separating the Light from the Darkness

The wisdom of the preceding ages is not sufficient fuel for Job's soul nor, seemingly, capable of ensuring his pathway to God: "Where is the way to the dwelling of light, and where is the place of darkness, that you may take it to its territory and that you may discern the paths to its home? You know, for you were born then, and the number of your days is great!" (38:19-21, RSV).

Separating light from darkness, from God's perspective, is a factor of being wise, yet Job finds his way to neither. Given the many years Job had lived, God questions how Job could not know. God's challenge to Job is that Job hasn't used the power that God has already awarded him, which renders Job virtually powerless in his complaining stupor.

Like Job, in our darkest hours, we struggle to find a sliver of light to grasp a bit of hope when our situations render us hopeless. Some of us live long enough to learn better within our circumstances, but often we dismiss the very wisdom that might provide light in our darkness or awareness in spaces where it feels like we cannot find God. Such places are where we wrestle with ourselves because of our dire straits yet strain to still have hope.

For Job, to speak without knowledge or to speak as though he was providing some counsel to God was unthinkable, but it signaled the very level of incredulity God reached when hearing Job's questions. God was having none of it. God's longevity far outstretches Job's or that of any of us—it is the difference between eternity and an earthly lifespan—even if Job, in his horror and haughtiness, was not fully ready to acknowledge that reality.

Imagine God asking Job, "Hey, dude, can you even measure the circumference of the earth?" Scripture records God asking Job, "Who determined its measurements—surely you know! Or who stretched the line upon it?" (38:5, RSV).

Signaling Job's comparable inadequacies, God answers God's own question, in essence saying, "You can't plumb the depths of my creation!" No one could be any clearer to those who might attempt to spar with God, regardless of their circumstances. Light and darkness factor greatly in Job's speeches—often as pseudonyms for good and evil or sin—and we find them both in God's responses as well: "Where does light come from, and where does darkness go? Can you take each to its home? Do you know how to get there?" (38:19-20, NLT).

God directly challenges Job's knowledge and his power over any portion of creation as well. If Job has no power over good and evil, nor any ability to impact light and darkness, then any discussion over any other aspect of creation is moot, including Job himself. God asks him, "Who has put wisdom in the inward parts, or given understanding to the mind?" (38:36, NRSV). Whether wrestling with life or with God, we humans are initially devoid of wisdom because we are not its source—God is!

But God's ultimate test is whether Job can successfully wrestle with Leviathan—a sea monster, whale, or crocodile. "Any hope of subduing it is false," says the Lord (41:9). So then, "no one is fierce enough to rouse it. Who then is able to stand against me? Who has a claim against me that I must pay? Everything under heaven belongs to me" (41:10-11). And God's conclusion of the matter is this: "Nothing on earth is its equal—a creature without fear. It looks down on all that are haughty; it is king over all that are proud" (41:33-34). Perhaps God made the Leviathan analogous to the struggle between Godself and Job in verbiage that Job could easily understand and grasp for his circumstances.

A God for All Our Circumstances

The Book of Job teaches us that if we construe God in terms of our circumstances, we stand on a shaky foundation. The quality of our spiritual lives depends not just on how we handle what happens to us but also on how we perceive it. If we construe our circumstances in terms of God's wisdom and character, which include *hesed* and *emeth* (steadfast love and faithfulness), we will not be shaken. God, after all, does not call us to understand all God's ways—God only calls us to trust in God. The pain of this life can push us beyond ourselves, beyond friends and family, into the arms of God, by causing us to realize that this world doesn't offer us sufficient wisdom. To help us cope, we eventually turn to the source of wisdom—God.

Concluding God's interrogatives toward Job, God comes to Job in a whirlwind, which in most other contexts suggests trouble or even destruction, but not for Job! Whirlwinds are certainly not the main context that God chose in which to address human concerns, but perhaps because of the juridical context of this story, God thinks it necessary to present Godself in this way. Other biblical references to whirlwinds tend to leave destruction in their wake like "a whirlwind sweeping in from the Negev" (Isaiah 21:1, NLT).

The suggestive power of whirlwinds is not to be mistaken; Elijah even journeyed to heaven on one! For Elijah's transport, the whirlwind became fuel for "a chariot of fire and horses of fire" (2 Kings 2:11). God's self-presentation to Job is no doubt quite stormy as God comes riding in on a whirlwind. However, God also comes in with a linguistic storm that garners Job's attention. God's response not only carries away Job's distress and anxiety "like chaff" (Isaiah 40:24) but is also a transforming power in Job's spiritual journey.

"Answer like the man you were called to be. Gird up your loins like a man (Hebrew: *geber*). Job is not asked to debase himself' he is called to present himself in all his vigor for the interchange . . ."[7]

God's faithfulness is such that it is not co-opted by the faithlessness of humanity; rather, it is a faithfulness grounded in God's omnipotence, omniscience, and omnipresence, which are on full display in this final scene with Job. We are assured through Job that God is not an "absentee landlord" but is intimately and continuously faithful to God's creation. Job's faith finds its moorings when facing the assurance and power of God's faithfulness! Though clothed in mystery, God is not *Deus absconditus*, or the "hidden God," any longer. God transforms this faithfully religious man into a man of faith supported by his religious practices. That is quite a personal and powerful transformation that now prepares Job for God's consequential blessings yet to come.

Before we read about the resolution to Job's story in the next chapter, I invite you to pause and reflect on the following questions.

Questions for Reflection and/or Response

1. Of the four possible frames in which the Book of Job suggests we picture our relationship with God, which one currently reflects your relationship with God?
2. How do we enlarge the frame?
3. What's your preferred source of wisdom?
4. God made sure that he got Job's attention through the whirlwind. In what ways does God capture your attention?

Notes

1. Raymond P. Scheindlin, *The Book of Job* (New York: Norton, 1999).
2. Walter Brueggemann, *Reverberations of Faith: A Theological Handbook of Old Testament Themes* (Louisville, KY: Westminster John Knox Press, 2002), 233.
3. James Strong, *Strong's Exhaustive Concordance of the Bible* (Peabody, MA: Hendrickson Publishers).
4. Brueggemann, 76.
5. Ibid., 201.
6. Garrett Green, *Imagining God* (Philadelphia: Fortress, 1989), 203.
7. J. Gerald Jansen, *Job: Interpretation, A Bible Commentary For Teaching and Preaching* (Atlanta: John Knox Press, 1985), 232.

Chapter Nine

JOB FINALLY SEES GOD (Job 42)

> Then Job replied to the LORD:
> "I know that you can do all things;
> no purpose of yours can be thwarted.
> You asked, 'Who is this that obscures my plans without
> knowledge?'
> Surely I spoke of things I did not understand,
> things too wonderful for me to know.
>
> You said, 'Listen now, and I will speak;
> I will question you,
> and you shall answer me.'
> My ears had heard of you
> but now my eyes have seen you.
> Therefore I despise myself
> and repent in dust and ashes."
>
> —42:2-6

Job's transformation is finally complete! Painful yet productive, Job's journey comes full circle. He reconciles some of his shattered relationships, and we know from the ending that he is blessed with new relationships, as he has another set of children. Of course, this does not lessen the sting of his previous losses, but he finds a path forward out of his pain and grief. What was religious adoration has now increased to awe over what Job sees of God, in contrast to what he merely heard from others. In all ways, Job overcomes every imaginable obstacle any human can face: the loss of his children and his wealth, health, status, and friends. Most of us never face all that Job did in one fell swoop, nor do we have our faith and relationship with God tested to the degree that Job endured.

Job went through quite a lot to be able to see God in a new way. From the verses above, consider how long he lived only hearing about God. His children were already adults, some of whom were living on their own, so Job was at least middle-aged by then. What was sufficient for him in the past was not sufficient for him as he wrestled with God in pursuit of a mature faith to sustain him in or pull him out of his pain and sorrow.

Hearing, Seeing, and Knowing

In 42:5 Job says to God, "My ears had heard of you but now my eyes have seen you." In your experience, what have you understood as the difference between *hearing about God* and *seeing* God? For some cultures where I have lived or had extended visits, hearing about anything or anyone is considered an inferior form of knowing, even rhetorically equivalent to not knowing.[1] For some people, hearing about something is not necessarily synonymous with knowing it; it may be only tantamount to a mere, superficial acquaintance with whatever or whomever the subject might be. To be clear, Job is not making a reference to his physical ears with this statement; he is simply identifying what his previous awareness of God was throughout the course of his life. He was aware of God and served God as that hearing or awareness dictated, but in seeing God, Job confirms that his relationship with God has gained new dimensions.

From my point of view, hearing represents awareness while seeing represents acceptance or engagement on some level. In my mind, hearing suggests a consciousness of something or someone while seeing attaches a value to some aspect of yourself through which meaning and substance can flow into your life. Generally, we don't automatically prioritize a matter just because we hear about it. People often declare, "Yeah, I heard about it, but I didn't *see* it," meaning that seeing tends to better validate whatever has happened. Therefore, compared to hearing about something, seeing tends to have some inherent value. What we are comfortable with only hearing about in our lives, rather than seeing, is deeply personal and highly selective, depending on our individual life situations.

From preachers to teachers to witness bearers of every stripe, we hear a lot about God. But little of it seems to impact us in a meaningful way until our circumstances become untenable. Think about a time in your life when harmful happenstances seemed to turn you inward and make you question all that you hold dear. These painful moments that are part of the human condition drive us to make sense of our existential condition, whether individually or collectively. In short, they urge us to seek God more fully.

My understanding of Job's seeing God is that it was tantamount to Job knowing God at a far more consequential level than he had previously experienced. From the verses at the beginning of this chapter, I envision that Job's religious journey to this point was like only hearing rumors or hearsay about God. Perhaps his spiritual connection lacked depth, though his religious commitment was evident because of his regular sacrifices to the deity he embraced. Have you ever felt that way—as if you are going through the motions of faith without feeling it? As Job came through his trials, his relationship with God was no longer defined by detachment or distance. His relationship was now imbued with a sense of affinity—a new clarity about God that he previously did not have. Sometimes the journey of seeking God in our times of trial leads us into a newly enriched relationship with God, like Job experienced.

Before his calamities, did Job have a pressing need to know his God up close and personal? As I read this biblical book, I sense that Job knew God primarily from a distance of sacrificial rites and rituals. Sometimes when we feel disconnected spiritually from God, we find ourselves going through the motions of familiar and comfortable rituals. Was this what had happened to Job? We know that Job engaged in daily religious activity through the offering of sacrifices, but did he have notable interaction with God before Satan's torment? He endured the suffering of boils; the death of his children, his workers, and his farm animals; the devastation of their houses, and denunciation by his friends. And he lamented that he could not find God (23:8).

When Job's sense of distance from God was so palpable, Job's priority was to seek God's face. Perhaps Job could not perceive at that time that God would find him even though no element of God's creation escapes God's love and attention.

We have no doubt that Job knew God and that his religious commitment was authentic. God was so assured of Job's commitment that God took up Satan's bet. However, an authentic commitment does not automatically create a deep sense of spiritual connection to God. Was that the case for Job? Due to Job's situation, we might understand that his life's contour required a powerful remolding, and only God had the power to successfully accomplish that. Job's friends, who had traveled from afar to comfort him, failed to remold the contours of Job's religious life because they couldn't convince him that his long-held beliefs were either wrong or inadequate. In my mind's eye, Job's knowledge of God seems like it might have been more scripted, academic, and ritualistic than personal. But he tenaciously held to it.

Truly knowing God is experiential and cannot be accomplished through academic or mental acuity alone. What elements do you bring to knowing and understanding God that go beyond study and reasoning? We need to bring our whole beings into our relationships with God—all human factors are involved in responsively focusing our lives on God while we quest for meaning and purpose. We must faithfully strive to integrate what we discover of the Creator into our daily lives.

Relating to God in Our Everyday Lives

H. Richard Niebuhr's book *Christ and Culture* greatly informs how I conceptualize how we relate to God in our daily lives. Culture can be defined as the context of our lives, while our chosen religion can be thought of as our way of making meaning within that context. How can we identify culture? We can think of it as the social life of any set of human beings, the environment they create in the areas of language, customs, habits, politics, ideas, beliefs, social organizations, values, inherited artifacts, and technical processes.[2]

Although people of various religions live in every corner of the world, all countries have a dominant, defining culture in which there is a corresponding majority religion. For example, in India, people will most likely be Hindu, and in Israel, people will most likely be Jewish, although religious minorities live in both countries. Many consider America to be a Christian country, with existing and the addition of other religions. Though thousands of different cultures exist globally, Niebuhr suggests that there are primarily four major ways in which most people relate to their deity and their culture. Using a Christian-influenced cultural frame, Niebuhr describes it as "opposition to culture (Christ against culture), agreement between Christ and culture (Christ of culture), a combination of both (Christ above culture), and tension between the kingdom of this world and the kingdom of heaven (Christ and culture in paradox) . . . which includes Christ, the Transformer of culture."[3]

Have you heard or considered some of these ideas when you have thought about the role of Christianity in our culture? They reflect the many-sided debate about the relationship between Christianity and civilization present in our time. Historians and theologians, statesmen and churchmen, Catholics and Protestants, Christians and non-Christians participate in it, and many voices are heard and many issues are raised. The question of Christianity and civilization is by no means a new one.[4]

Niebuhr cites the work of Rabbi Abraham Klausner, in his chapter "The Enduring Problem" describing how the "problem of Jesus and culture" must have appeared to the Pharisees and Sadducees. He defended their repudiation of the Nazarene on the grounds that Jesus imperiled Jewish civilizations and that, culturally, Judaism and Christianity have been wrestling with this problem. Klausner shares that Judaism is not only a religion or an ethical framework but also the sum of the nation's needs placed into a religious context. In other words, Judaism is a national life—a life that includes the national religion and a set of human ethical principles that embrace without engulfing.[5] Perhaps we see some of this interplay through Job's story in the Hebrew Bible.

Within such contexts, we move from culture toward God, questing for meaning and purpose. Then we draw from our relationship with God to provide our culture with the best that relationship affords. People who practice different religions have diverse views on how to incorporate their religion and social structures into their lives and how to express their religion and culture to the wider world. This tension between culture and religious expression existed within and between humans long before Christianity, Judaism, Hinduism, Islam, or the religions from Job's era. All human beings, within their ethnicities, nationalities, and economic or educational statuses, make decisions about religious practice in their daily lives that shape their lives, their groups, and their world. I have been fortunate to have traveled to more than forty countries on four different continents, and the vastly different ways in which people engage in their religions and apply the principles of those religions, personally and collectively, to their earthly domains is nothing short of amazing.

We are defined by the degree to which we allow religion to determine the contours of our lives and culture. Job's day was no different from our own. What differences do you observe in the ways his friends presented their culture and faith? Think for a moment about the differences you see between people and how they integrate culture and religion. Do you observe idiosyncratic differences that are as unique as personalities or political preferences? We live on the same human continuum as Job and his friends. The variation of individual religious intensity or commitment depends on the degree to which we quest for meaning and value in our lives and thereby choose to shape our culture. That intensity either narrows or broadens the religious "distance" between an individual and his or her god(s) or the commitment and practices that eventually define that person's life.

Within Christianity, followers can range from being nominal Christians to being deeply dedicated. Some are deeply knowledgeable about Scripture, while others are minimally aware. Some individuals identify more as "cultural Christians," whose lives are managed primarily by cultural tenets rather than their faith. We might be able to imagine that Job's realization that he was satisfied previously with having only heard about God was something like "cultural Christianity." Can we picture how Job's suffering redeemed his enquiring mind to the point of seeing God and moving from cultural religion to a more spiritually connected faith?

Questions Deepen Faith

As we gain an understanding of Job's journey, the questions that unsettle our faith can serve to deepen it as well. Questions about our faith can help us be in touch with a vibrantly patterned process that allows us to make life spiritually meaningful. Such questions help us reflect on the center of value and power that can sustain our lives. Through these questions, we find coherence in and give meaning to the force that created and sustains our lives. Job's questions confirmed that because of his suffering, he had to find a way to make life worth living again. As humans, we look for something to love that loves us, something to value that gives us value, and something to honor and respect that holds us in high esteem as well. And when we find the love, honor, and esteem we crave from the one we love, honor, and esteem, we, like Job, are transformed from only hearing about God to finally seeing the God who pours love, honor, and power back into our lives after it has been drained out of us because of painful, even diabolical, circumstances and afflictions.

Job's Repentance

In chapter 42, we see that Job successfully came through the tests Satan designed and God allowed, just as God anticipated he would. God's questioning of Job ushers in a sense of awe that ignites Job's repentance and narrows the spiritual distance between them. Through his traumas, Job trades the ritualistic distance between him and God for richer reverence on which his repentance hinged. The act of repentance became the experience that opened the door to a much improved and deeper relationship with God. Once stripped of his earthly possessions, children, workers, and pretensions, Job learns to appreciate being an infinitesimal part of a beloved creation but beloved nonetheless by a holy God. Job's struggles transform the value of his relationships while simultaneously opening his capacity to see God. God's lengthy interrogation forced Job to grasp his own human inadequacy relative to the grand universe that God revealed to him.

The Significance of Job Today

The Book of Job offers a special significance for us today and serves as a guide that can inspire a more meaningful relationship with God and a more purpose-filled life in this world. Whether God touches our tangible possessions or the intangibles of our beings, God does not fail in any of it that might awaken us to God. How wonderful to know that regardless of the many changes life puts us through, mirrored in Job's experiences, we serve a God who is unchangeable. Job held to what he believed about God in the face of blistering verbal assaults from his friends. Are there times in your life when you have been strengthened by clinging to your beliefs even when friends questioned you? We can use Job's example as inspiration to stay true to God through thick and thin. And we can be assured that the immutable God is with us through it.

Famed psychologist Carl Jung shared his interpretations of the Book of Job and its role in contemporary life. He observed, "These experiences [like Job's] come upon [us humans] from inside as well as from outside, and it is useless to interpret them rationalistically and thus weaken them by apotropaic [the power to avert evil influences or bad luck] means."[6] Jung said that the key differences between human nature and God's nature began with Adam and Eve and progressed to God as presented in the Book of Revelation. Jung said God was preparing humankind for the transition from the Old Testament Yahweh image to the fallen Christ. From Jung's perspective, Job stood as a prefiguration of the Christ of the Gospels, which is a central theme in Jung's *Answer to Job*.[7] If we read this book with a high Christology, as Jung does, perhaps we can see parallels between the unjust suffering of Job, Jesus, and ourselves. Through Jesus, we understand that God is sympathetic to human suffering and has also experienced it through Christ. God understands our suffering firsthand.

What a glorious transformation for Job and us when we realize how deep God's care for humanity runs, even when dire straits challenge us. At the end of the book, we see that Job declared that these experiences affirmed his beliefs. The truths he held about God withstood Satan's test. Once Job's beliefs were confirmed, God reopened Job's life for the restoration Job wanted.

One thing often overlooked is that God not only restored community for Job but welcomed back Job's brothers and sisters into Job's life, who are not even mentioned earlier in the book: "All his brothers and sisters and everyone who had known him before came and ate with him in his house. They comforted and consoled him over all the trouble the LORD had brought on him, and each one gave him a piece of silver and a gold ring" (42:11).

Job's siblings and his community folk came to reaffirm and celebrate him even before his personal family was restored. This was a celebration engineered by the highest authority: God.

In the next chapter, we will read more about how Job's life began anew following his many trials. Before we celebrate God's blessings along with Job, I invite you to pause for reflection on the following questions.

Questions for Reflection and/or Response

1. What element(s) of your culture can you identify as essential in the religion you embrace?
2. Against what do you test your beliefs?
3. After hearing about God, what life experience or moment of reality has allowed you to "see God"?
4. What was the transforming moment, or experience, between your "hearing about God" and "seeing God with your own eyes," as Job describes his personal experience? Relative to people, distinguish between "hearing about" and "seeing" them.

Notes

1. Raymond P. Scheindlin, *The Book of Job* (New York: Norton, 1999), 222.
2. H. Richard Niebuhr, *Christ and Culture* (San Francisco: Harper, 2001).
3. Ibid., 3–10.
4. Ibid., 3.
5. Abraham Klausner, cited in Niebuhr.
6. Carl Gustav Jung, *Answer to Job* (Zurich: Racher Verlag, 1952), 2.
7. Jung, 3.

Chapter Ten

LIFE BECOMES NEW AGAIN

For Job, the old is gone, and the new has arrived. Job triumphs. We can sigh with relief that Job survived the harsh tribulations and devastating trials inflicted upon him as a test. Being completely unaware of what triggered his suffering undoubtedly made it even more traumatic. Because we often know the cause of our own suffering or calamities, we might sympathize with Job, who knew nothing of the cause of his crises.

From Tried to Triumphant

Job's lack of awareness about Satan's role in the crises is a masterful literary tool that creates intrigue and allows the reader to connect more deeply with the victim. Job's unawareness about the cause of his suffering was part of the plan; his not knowing inflicted its own pain. As Thomas Oden wrote, "Job, who in his extraordinary temperance and celebrated faith became poor from rich, despised from illustrious, ugly from attractive, [and] ill from healthy, is proposed to us as a model of patient faith."[1] But in the end, the physical pains were gone, and all that he lost was restored.

While Job and his wife continued to bear the pain of losing their adult children, new children came into their lives, creating new relationships. Job's fellowship with God is renewed, his relationship with God within the human realm is redefined, and his world celebrates with him from his house to the city gate. Bernhard Anderson comments, "Although Job finds no access from man to God, he dares to hope that someday, somehow, a reconciliation will take place."[2] Often, we do not know how frail we are until tragedy or trauma strikes. Such events reroute life and often lend us few options with which to get our lives back on track. Our way forward may not come from a doctor, a judge, or even a friend, but it is always possible through our faith—through an intimate relationship with God.

Job's persistent querying with God helped him weather the storm. That persistence brought him through the worst of his life into the best and most powerful moment, in which he sees God. Such new sight is often fostered by a faith that has been shaped by more questions than answers. *Faith must be tried before it is triumphant.* Although we most likely won't have to endure trials like we read in this biblical book, our own trials and tribulations can be no less gut-wrenching and unbelievably daunting. God allows our testing, not for God to discover what we believe or how devout we are, but so that we might know that we stand on solid ground in our faith. Such faith ignites our continued confidence in God, keeping us open to God's strength, direction, and comfort, which both smooths our way and eases the pain.

As Satan was prosecuting Job in the divine courtroom, God called Job his servant. God was confident in Job's ability to stay the course and to remain faithful to the covenant that evidently was in place. God knew what God had made and how it would function even amid the diabolical efforts to de-create a specimen of God's created masterpiece of humanity. Now Job is elevated from just a servant or friend of God to the role of a priest. He is now responsible for hearing the pleas for forgiveness from his friends, and then making such pleas right with God with a sacrificial offering on their behalf. The friends had to bring the bull (no double entendre intended) that would be offered to God on their behalf. Eliphaz the Temanite, Bildad the Shuhite, and Zophar the Naamathite did what the Lord told them so that Job could make that sacrificial offering and pray for them because they had verbally accosted and diminished Job, or as we say, called him everything but a child of God. How beautiful that the Lord accepted Job's prayers on behalf of his friends (42:10).

We must reflect on Job's journey for a moment. It began with what Bernhard Anderson calls "one of the most poignant passages in the Bible [because] it expresses the aching misery of existence in language of rare imaginative power."[3] This prayer encompassed Job's lament. Many of us cringe when we hear the word *lament* because we only intuit the sorrow or anguish it entails without realizing that hope is woven into that process. Yes, Job was angry and deeply sorrowful. He even cursed the moment he was conceived, but it was all within the context of his relationship with God, for Job confessed, "I know that my Redeemer (Hebrew *goel*) lives" (19:25). So, because Job's lament was within the context of his relationship with God, Job was not empty of hope. That sliver of hope seemed to usher him in awe toward the God he sought to serve.

Job's Model of Faith Development

Not only do I discern a faith development process in the Book of Job, but I also observe that the ability to powerfully lament becomes the very infrastructure of that developing faith—a lament that flows staccato-like from Job's soul. In Job, we witness the paradox of both pain and promise. Such laments can bring change not just to our hearts but also to our culture.

In this treasured biblical book, we watch Job go from lament to awe to prayer to faith to forgiveness to reconciliation to community—an incredible journey for anyone! Can you identify those elements within your own faith journey? How have you walked the path from lament to awe to prayer to faith and forgiveness? These steps do not happen overnight. They either result from stimuli to our spiritual growth or are themselves stimuli. Such spiritual growth drivers can result from a new encounter or, conversely, could possibly be driven by a deep conscious desire. These are the stones that paved Job's path, assuring his faithfulness and leading to a celebration that embraced the totality of his life: from friends to flocks and from family to faith—everything and everyone is included in celebrating his having survived the diabolical efforts to de-create what the Creator placed not only as the "centerpiece" of his creation but also as the sole authority of creation under him! Mark Vroegop encourages us, as faithful Bible readers, to become "fluent in lament, the historic prayer language of processing and expressing grief."[4]

From Lament to Awe

David McKenna said, "Job's restoration is essential to [the] message [of the book], not for Job's personal prosperity, but for Job's spiritual prosperity."[5] When, like Job, we raise our questions to God, the inherent reality is that we will not only know that God exists but that God can answer the very questions we ask. The abundance of such questions and assertions interspersed with words of praise and confidence, help to shore up a sense of awe in Job and in us. "God has made my heart faint; the Almighty has terrified me. Yet I am not silenced by the darkness, by the thick darkness that covers my face" (23:16-17).

No fear could silence Job. No lack of assurance in the darkest period of his life could negate the relationship he had with the Almighty who terrified him. Nor could it force him to flee. Through it all, Job clung to the one whom he knew could answer his questions, even if in the moment God refused to provide Job with the answers he was seeking. As David McKenna comments,

> In response to Job's repentance in dust and ashes, God shows him his love and bestows his grace. Even though Job has nothing to offer God and God owes him nothing but justice, he rises from the ash heap forgiven, accepted, and restored by God. . . . How do we know Job is forgiven, accepted, and restored by God? The confirmation is in the grace that Job shares with his foes, his friends, and his family. Grace received is grace to be given.[6]

After Bildad sought to diminish Job, a "praise report" flowed from Job's mouth. Job listed just a few of God's accomplishments as though Bildad knew little about the power that God displays throughout creation. Job declared, "Behold, these are but the outskirts of his ways, and how small a whisper do we hear of him! But the thunder of his power who can understand?" (26:14, ESV). Job was saying that if what you've been spouting is all you know about God, then you are only on the outskirts of understanding who God is. Essentially, Bildad and the other friends were not close enough to God to discern God's very essence. This is another poignant moment in which Job confirmed his awe for God, especially in contrast to what he believed was present in his friends!

From Awe to Reverence and Humility

In his book *Thirty Days of Liberation*, Rabbi Michael Rose Knopf informs us that "faith matters . . . [and that] faith demands the presence of doubt, the capacity to affirm the limits of what we know. And only through such intellectual humility can we be free to honor others' truths and to be compassionate in the application of our own."[7] Among other evidence of his fervent praying, perhaps Job was reaching that point when he said, "My face is red with weeping, dark shadows ring my eyes; yet my hands have been free of violence and my prayer is pure" (16:16-17).

He was in touch with God in ways not previously realized. Job's praying was intense, as the following verses confirm: "And after my skin has been destroyed, yet in my flesh I will see God; I myself will see him with my own eyes—I, and not another. How my heart yearns within me!" (19:26-27).

Job's fervent hope served him well as it ignited such fundamental anticipation. Though ravaged by disease, Job experienced a yearning for God, who seemed to be at a great distance that only his questions seemed to reach. But Job pressed in his search, which allowed his nascent faith to span the distance he perceived between himself and God. Job found God! The God he previously questioned responded to his awe and reverence, and his fervent prayers became the generator of his new faith—his new ability and experience of seeing God with his own eyes.

From Prayer to Faith

God confirmed what Job discerned about the friends' relationship with God and that much of what they said about God was incorrect. What these friends declared about God, including their beliefs or assessment of God, did not please God one iota. God even said, "Not true" further confirming Job's own previous religious assessment of his friends, that is, that they were just "on the 'outskirts' of who God is." "After the Lord had said these things to Job, he said to Eliphaz the Temanite, 'I am angry with you and your two friends, because you have not spoken the truth about me, as my servant Job has'" (42:7).

Despite the incorrect information the friends had dumped on Job, none of it soaked into his spirit, which helped him to remain free to search for God in his own way. These expressions of awe seasoned Job to be tapped by God to pray for those who did not speak the truth about God or might not have known God at all. After all that Job suffered at their hands, God appointed Job to become their intercessor. Through the faith wrought by the questions lofted toward God from Job's soul, Job was ready to pray—readied by God—even to intercede on behalf of others. That divine assignment opened the door to forgiveness, the possibility of which was generated by Job's newly found faith.

From Faith to Forgiveness

Prayer conditions us to forgive and creates the very channel through which the power to forgive flows through us into the lives of others. But the generating power behind prayer is our faith. Job's friends were ready to bring the bulls and rams as a sacrifice to God, but that sacrifice was not acceptable to God until Job prayed for Bildad, Zophar, and Eliphaz. Job then implored God to forgive them:

> After the LORD had spoken these words to Job, the LORD said to Eliphaz the Temanite: "My anger burns against you and against your two friends, for you have not spoken of me what is right, as my servant Job has. Now therefore take seven bulls and seven rams and go to my servant Job and offer up a burnt offering for yourselves. And my servant Job shall pray for you, for I will accept his prayer not to deal with you according to your folly. For you have not spoken of me what is right, as my servant Job has." (42:7-8, ESV)

The inability to forgive takes its toll on many relationships, but the need to be forgiven and to forgive permeates our relationship with the Creator and with one another. For God to accept Job's prayer for the three friends was God's confirmation of forgiving them. While rejoicing about the extraordinary blessings Job received in the end, we might overlook the blessings these friends received at that moment: restored and renewed friendship with Job and with God. Perhaps the compassion that stirred their initial desire to comfort him was also reignited. As a result of this prayer, God wiped the slate clean, freeing them from the baggage they would have carried had forgiveness not been offered and received.

From Forgiveness to Reconciliation

Can you imagine how painful it must have been for Job to have experienced not only spiritual distance from God but also the painful disparagement he received constantly from his friends? For most of the Book of Job, we experience no sense of community in what his friends share. These friends were adversarial toward Job, thus hindering any sense of connection they may have previously enjoyed. Naturally, Job sustained moral injuries to his psyche and soul, which caused his life to devolve into darkness, creating his need for even just a sliver of light again, representing the *hope* he longed for. Throughout his speeches, Job's quest was for a new moral surety beyond his lost life.

For many years, I have been teaching a four-session study I developed on forgiveness. From my experience, I have no doubt in my mind that forgiving is one of the most difficult tasks God has ever required of us mere humans. Some folks I've met would rather climb Mount Everest barefoot than forgive anyone who has seriously offended them. Part of the reason it is difficult for many to forgive is that the world misleads us by saying, "If you haven't forgotten, you haven't forgiven." But this is not the case at all. Forgetting is impossible! Forgiving is possible. In reality, the task is letting go of the pain.

Although Job's three friends impugned his reputation throughout and misled him about God, when God told Job to forgive them, it wasn't about forgetting. Rather, forgiveness was simply opening the relational door to reconciliation with him and with each other. Forgiveness was an invitation to shalom, which as Soong-Chan Rah says, "embraces the suffering of others as an instrumental aspect of well-being.

Shalom requires lament."[8] And it is lament that for us, individually and collectively, propels us toward awe, which results in prayer and provides the power to forgive. Reconciliation leads us into community, which is the blessing that God restored to Job, his friends, and his family.

From Reconciliation to Community

"After Job had prayed for his friends, the LORD restored his fortunes and gave him twice as much as he had before. All his brothers and sisters and everyone who had known him before came and ate with him in his house. They comforted and consoled him over all the trouble the LORD had brought on him, and each one gave him a piece of silver and a gold ring" (42:10-11). "And everyone who had known him before came and ate with him" confirms that Job experienced a renewed sense of community that included those who had previously been serious religious combatants. But look at what lament achieved for Job by the grace of God! Imagine how lament can shape our lives. Life in God, at its best, is far beyond whatever context might temporarily characterize our lives. Such life must rise to the level of community because we are communal beings by nature; the best of who we are and what we can be is found in community.

Job's life was reestablished with his friends, siblings, and wider community members because he reconciled with God and others. Repentance and reconciliation through forgiveness was the path that God specifically carved out for Job to usher him out of the darkness Job detested and into the light for which he longed. Evidently Job's siblings and extended family were never touched by Job's tragedies. We might ask why this was the case: Did they not live close by? Had they never heard the chatter about him at the gate of the city where Job used to congregate with others? In these verses, we read that they celebrated with him with a family dinner, bringing gifts of silver and gold to rejoice in his release from the darkness of his diabolical experiences. It is amazing that their existence is not mentioned at the beginning of the book, as we only hear about Job's wife and children and not Job's siblings. I do not think this suggests any discord but it was perhaps because they did not live in proximity to Job. We do not hear of their existence until Job's restoration. That lends credence to the idea that this is a literary account of a real person, which allows for some details to be edited and some weighty details to be omitted. The siblings' absence from the story's beginning does not change the story; however, their presence at the end of the story heightens both Job's joy and ours. Job's siblings are part of God's blessings upon Job and his household.

Pastor Rick Warren has said, "There is no growth without change; there is no change without loss; there is no loss without grief; and there is no grief without pain."[9] As we have read, through all his change, loss, grief, and pain, Job never cursed God as Satan declared he would. On the contrary, Job clearly voices his indisputable faith in God.

How intriguing that God not only restored what Job had lost, but he added extra to those blessings by doubling what Job had lost. Could that possibly relate to the second round of suffering that Satan caused by adding an additional test of Job's dedication to God? God did not increase the number of daughters, but their beauty was noteworthy as God doubled Job's other blessings. God simply added a quality that would continue to bring praise and honor to the house of Job because "nowhere in all the land were there found women as beautiful as Job's daughters" (42:15).

The gift of Job's seven sons was considered an ideal number; likewise, Job's three daughters signal to all what Francis Anderson describes as "the completeness and divine approval that God lavished upon Job."[10] In order, the daughters are named Jemimah, Keziah, and Keren-Happuch (42:14). We would be remiss to ignore that their father granted them an inheritance along with their brothers. Though this was more the historical exception than the rule, there was equality in Job's house before inequality became the social and political norm through which women in many parts of the world are disenfranchised.

Job's restoration is now complete, and God grants Job many more years of life to enjoy these doubled blessings in abundance: "Job lived a hundred and forty years; he saw his children and their children to the fourth generation. And so Job died, an old man and full of years" (42:16-17). Did the new life with new children remove the painful loss of their first children? Probably not—but the blessings of life after loss helped Job reconcile and enjoy a long life after that great trauma.

In the next chapter, we will consider the role of lament in the church's understanding of God's forgiveness and peace. Before we do so, I invite you to pause and reflect on the following questions.

Questions for Reflection and/or Response

1. Describe the sense of awe you experience or enjoy individually and/or in worship.
2. How easy is it for you to forgive?
3. What can the ability to lament do for you?
4. Other than by God, what is it like to be forgiven? Share a meaningful example.
5. Have you ever reconciled with someone who deeply offended you?
6. How easy is it today to find a sense of community?

Notes

1. Thomas C. Oden, ed., *Ancient Christian Commentary on Scripture* (Downers Grove, IL: InterVarsity, 2019), xviii.
2. Bernhard W. Anderson, *Understanding the Old Testament*, 3rd ed. (Englewood Cliffs, NJ: Prentice Hall, 1975), 557.

3. Ibid.
4. Mark Vroegop, *Weep with Me: How Lament Opens the Door for Racial Reconciliation* (Wheaton, IL: Crossway, 2020), 22.
5. David L. McKenna, *Job*, The Communicator's Commentary (Waco, TX: Word, 1986), 321.
6. Ibid.
7. Michael Knopf, *Thirty Days of Liberation: Pathways for Personal and Social Transformation Inspired by the Book of Exodus* (independently published, 2020).
8. Soong-Chan Rah, *Prophetic Lament: A Call for Justice in Troubled Times* (Downers Grove, IL: InterVarsity, 2015).
9. Rick Warren, "God Grows You One Step at a Time," PastorRick.com, July 15, 2021, https://pastorrick.com/god-grows-you-one-step-at-a-time/.
10. Francis I. Anderson, *Job: An Introduction and Commentary*, Tyndale Old Testament Commentaries (Downers Grove, IL: InterVarsity, 2008), 14:79.

Chapter Eleven

TO MOVE FROM CHAOS TO COMMUNITY, THE CHURCH MUST LAMENT

Throughout this book, we have witnessed Job's lamenting as integral to his journey through religion toward faith in God whom he could now see with new spiritual eyes. They pave his way from the darkness of despair toward the light of hope. However, I believe Job's journey from tried to triumphant can also serve as a guide for the church today. After all, the church has experienced some spiritual losses and financial threats to its health and well-being over the past few years. We've lost generations of believers to the "nones" and "dones."[1] At the church level, could this feel similar to the loss of Job's adult children? Churches around the nation lost cherished members to the COVID-19 pandemic—not only in the deaths of members but also through membership losses following mandated church closures. The loss of people and resources has decimated many congregations' fiscal health. With so much taken from us, so to speak, perhaps we, as the church, might find ourselves similarly tried like Job.

We can understand, then, from the Book of Job, that for us as the church to reach restoration and reconciliation with

God, we must learn and engage in lamenting before God and with one another. That we must lament is both hard and good news. Job found no peace in sitting on his ash heap in silence for seven days. He found no solace in simple introspection. When he began to consider himself in relation to the Creator, the one to whom he owed his life, he tapped into a sense of awe that would lead him to new discoveries in that relationship. Similarly, the church will not find peace just by rehashing sad sagas as we sit in our pain on our own ash heap, bemoaning the lost glory days when our Sunday schools were full and our budgets were robust. Can we follow Job's example and consider afresh what our Lord yet calls the church to be?

Within the depth and breadth of my forty years in ministry as clergy, the church has identified the root or source of every problem outside of itself. However, have we neglected the core of who we are? When I contemplate who we are as the church, three verses immediately come to mind:

> Therefore go and make disciples of all nations, baptizing them in the name of the Father and of the Son and of the Holy Spirit, and teaching them to obey everything I have commanded you. And surely I am with you always, to the very end of the age. (Matthew 28:19-20)

> For we were all baptized by one Spirit so as to form one body—whether Jews or Gentiles, slave or free—and we were all given the one Spirit to drink. (1 Corinthians 12:13)

> So, in Christ we, though many, form one body, and each member belongs to all the others. (Romans 12:5)

Think about these verses as you consider the state of the church today. We go inside to worship, but once we're outside the sanctuary doors, we divide what Christ united. The

Reverend Dr. Martin Luther King Jr. famously lamented that eleven o'clock Sunday morning is one of the most, if not *the* most, segregated hours in Christian America.[2] Though efforts have been made to move beyond racial and cultural divisions, sometimes those divisions feel deeper and more prevalent today than they were decades ago during the Civil Rights era, with contempt for each other being stoked by some politicians and clergy alike.

The Church's Lament

Our culture seems to have suppressed, eroded, supplanted, diminished, or even eliminated what God in Christ Jesus created when he walked this earth. If you ask some folk about the condition of the church today, they will often respond with a list of negative comments such as:

> "It's all about the Benjamins!"
> "Oh, it's just one big production!"
> "The preacher this or that."
> "It's more like entertainment."
> "They don't do anything (or do so little) for the community!"

The good news is that whatever is wrong with the church is fixable but not without making the time and the space to lament appropriately. Sometimes it seems like the spiritual power that has been given to the church is overshadowed by a quest for worldly powers: political power, racial supremacy, and economic dominance. But this does not account for the great variety of abuses under church and cathedral roofs! The collective church has plenty for which to lament. However, we should remember that simply complaining is not the same as lamenting. Lamenting is not just an excuse to utter one's complaints. We are not asking for anyone's personal list of grievances, because those are usually about someone else instead of one's own self. For the church to lament, we must face the depth of reality of how we have failed our Lord, and then pour out our souls in repentance:

> Hatred and contempt are growing faster than love.
> Money is our measure more than missions.
> Growth in the number of members is more important than growing in faith.

This list only identifies a few failures over which we need to lament. Through reflection perhaps we might gain the humility to be remorseful in our failures and honest enough to acknowledge our need to lament. Lamentation and repentance open the church up not just for change but for a mature and more substantive faith that can yet empower us to be the church our Lord bequeathed to us as a source of healing for our world.

Historically the church has lamented for others—it is past time for the church to lament for itself. Many who were driven from their churches by the pandemic have not returned. Some have found other Christian, spiritual, or religious resources. Could it be that these former parishioners and church members never had opportunities to engage in lament as an aspect of Sunday or Wednesday worship, so they found that freedom at home? The invocation or morning prayer does not relish a lament from its worship leaders or the one offering prayer during an altar call. A few years ago, I was frequently asked to do the Sunday morning altar call in a congregation where I assisted the pastor. After more than a year, he said to me, "You pray too long." (I wondered why he so frequently called on me to pray!) As part of my prayer practice, I lamented before God so worshippers would be spiritually refreshed not only with a sense of awe but also be able to see God—and themselves—with fresh eyes.

In my many readings of Job, I have found evidence of a spiritual and social movement that Job may have been unaware of, forming within him until his intervening moments with God. In this book that I so deeply treasure, I easily see connections between Job's awe, prayer, forgiveness, reconciliation with friends, and renewed sense of community, as well as his travail, which fueled his lamenting. Of the Ten Commandments, not one says, "Thou shalt lament." However, the need for and ability to lament clearly emerged in the life of the Hebrew nation as a function of their worship not only because of the difficulties they experienced. With stories like Job and Jonah, an entire book dedicated to Lamentations, and a major holiday dedicated to atonement, Christianity's Judaic forebears clearly understood the role of lament in their relationship with God.

The Relationship between Confession and Lament

With few general exceptions, we American Christians neither face nor endure persecution as a backlash to our faith. Our position within the fabric of the dominant culture provides a certain level of comfort and security. Yet, within our prayer lives, have we felt the need to lament before God? Soong-Chan Rah describes what it means to lament: "Laments are prayers of petition arising out of need. But lament is not simply the presentation of a list of complaints, nor merely the expression of sadness over difficult circumstances. Lament in the Bible is a liturgical response to the reality of suffering and engages God in the context of pain and trouble."[3]

Lament is not just praying about the happenstances of oneself, friends, relatives, members of one's congregation, or the community who may have fallen on hard times. It is not simply bearing down in prayer about problems. Rather, as Rah continues: "[Lament includes] repentance and confession—not simply offered for individual sins but also for the sins of community. To move from the place of lament to the possibility of restoration, confession needs to be a part of the equation. Confession cannot be skipped in lament in order to get to the quick and easy solutions."[4]

In my Baptist tradition, confession would be an unusual element of worship. Some Protestant traditions include a corporate prayer of confession followed by an assurance of pardon, but do we consciously experience lament as a part of these prayers? Most Protestants do not practice auricular confession, like the Catholic tradition of confessing sins to a priest to receive forgiveness. However, we should understand that confession is the essence of a lament and that it is not just a stand alone, individual practice. In our failure to be the church Christ has called us to be, there is much for which we need to lament!

While we find no confessions in Job's speeches, we can see that he clearly was aware of sin. Though he "shunned evil" (1:1) and was a man of integrity who offered sacrifices for his children's possible sins, he must have been aware of his own as well. His confessions were likely part and parcel of his worship in which he offered daily sacrifices to God. Consider these words from Psalm 130 as an example of the Judaic worshipful inclusion of confession:

> Out of the depths I cry to you, LORD;
> Lord, hear my voice.
> Let your ears be attentive
> to my cry for mercy.
>
> If you, LORD, kept a record of sins,
> Lord, who could stand?
> But with you there is forgiveness,
> so that we can, with reverence, serve you.
>
> —verses 1-4

Beyond personal sins or grief, the church needs to lament over its collective sins and grief concerning the obvious conditions of this world. Many church leaders are calling for the church to lament within corporate worship. The Reverend Dr. Tesia Mallory, dean of the chapel at United

Theological Seminary, speaks to the struggles she perceives within congregations:

> It's crucial that we as church leaders make space in our worship services for our congregants to lament before God. Corporate lament is a powerful tool that gives people permission to grieve and name their fears, doubts, and deepest longings before the Lord. The scriptures, especially the Psalms, are full of expressions of lament both personal and communal. [Leaders should] . . . make room for grief and . . . ask God to fill us by the power of the Holy Spirit to be agents of change in the world.[5]

In our journey through Job, we perceive that personal confession and laments can support the development of a healthier spiritual life and a deeper relationship with God, but it can also serve to spiritually cleanse and enliven the congregation. Now that we have looked at the case for common confession and lament as the church community, let's consider how these elements that so beautifully nourished Job's journey could serve the church of today.

From Lament to Awe

Having examined Job's spiritual movement through forty-two chapters, I believe there is a clear way to proceed: we begin with *lament*, which produces *awe* and opens us up to prayer. Prayer requires *forgiveness* to find *reconciliation* that blossoms into *community*. This is an incredible journey at both a personal and communal level. In the story of Job, much of this happens in the last chapter. However, the seeds and capacities were planted and enabled long before the book begins. I believe that lament is not a step to be missed, as it helps produce and sustain a sense of community, which is the oneness for which Jesus prayed in John 17: "My prayer is not for them alone. I pray also for those who will believe in me through their message, that all of them may be one, Father, just as you are in me and I am in you. May they also be in us so that the world may believe that you have sent me" (verses 20-22).

In Job 42, we see God sever Job's friends from their antagonistic attitude toward Job. God literally cleans away that sinfulness with required offerings and the necessity of forgiveness. Now, before you rush out to buy a bull or two, just reread John 17, and you will grasp that our horrid past has already been cleansed. Jesus' prayer frees us to move toward that earthly goal of community. But *our* role now is to engage in cleansing moments of lament and prayer.

From Awe to Prayer

Can we rediscover the transcendence of God both within our own lives and within the lives of our churches from just our music selections, brief invocations, or momentary altar calls? The worship experience should remind worshippers of the sense of awe we should have in the name of the Lord. Often our prayers become a "bless us" or "help us" for whatever the need of the day might be. Do our prayers contain the profusion of praise and adoration that the God and Savior whom we are there to worship deserve? Turning the focus to God does not mean that we care any less for folks by not calling their names in prayer in our sanctuaries. But while praying in worship, we sometimes focus far more on our physical needs than on the God we are there to worship. We need to extol and adore God, not just beg God for favors or blessings. Has our worship behavior in the church now led many parishioners to spiritually self-medicate? Could this contribute to the reason that after the COVID years, significant numbers are not returning to their churches?

From Prayer to Repentance

Prayer should first and foremost exalt God. When our prayers become too focused on ourselves, whether individually or as a congregation, we can lose sight of that primary purpose. Prayer for those on the sick list and for the budget has its place, but it should not be the central focus. We gather to *worship*, not just to list our struggles and needs. Sometimes our prayers in church seem more perfunctory than an effort to inspire worshippers and transcend our natural setting.

Sometimes I wonder if we teach more about what God *does* than who God *is*. Yes, God put food on our table. Yes, God blessed you with a new job. Yes, God healed you and woke you up this morning. But who is God beyond our physical needs? Who is God beyond our present circumstances? Job captured the transcendence of God. How do we incorporate that transcendence into our worship, infusing into worshippers the power necessary to have a meaningful impact on our families, our community, and our world as God grants us such opportunities? Our worship is not just lifting up "holy hands"; it is an opportunity to bless and give glory to the Lord, rather than primarily asking God to pour us out a blessing. What welcomes the holy into worship that might lead us to repentance? The moments when God is exalted! Recall this verse from Isaiah: "Remember the former things, those of long ago; I am God, and there is no other; I am God, and there is none like me" (46:9). That is why and whom we worship—a reality to which the church needs to return!

Having worshipped in churches in many parts of the world and listened to prayers in a variety of worship services, sometimes it seems as if the person praying envisions a god who is "out there somewhere." Some seem to pray to a god who is "over there" but who will come and meet our needs. In such moments, I wonder if the sense of transcendence is lost and if listeners begin to silently focus on their own needs, whether spoken or not. For if the sense of transcendence is lost, our worship becomes more vain and vapid. In times like these, do we adequately capture the awareness in prayer that God is not only in us but that we are in God? Consider the following verses:

> "For in him we live and move and have our being." As some of your own poets have said, "We are his offspring." (Acts 17:28)

> Know therefore that the LORD your God is God; he is the faithful God, keeping his covenant of love to a thousand generations of those who love him and keep his commands. (Deuteronomy 7:9)

These verses remind us of our position in God, as well as of the importance of awe in our worship.

Repentance Ushers in Forgiveness

Many people seem not to know how to forgive, or they believe that forgiveness is impossible. The world has convinced them that revenge, backbiting, or othering is more advantageous to them. When we engage in these behaviors, we desacralize what the Bible holds as sacrosanct: "If you forgive those who sin against you, your heavenly Father will forgive you. But if you refuse to forgive others, your Father will not forgive your sins" (Matthew 6:14-15, NLT). The openness we bring to God is the reason God grants us the power to forgive! In more than fifteen years of teaching my four-session Bible study on forgiveness, I have discovered in people not only a lack of knowledge of how to forgive, but more significantly, an unwillingness or outright obstinacy in the face of this biblical requirement. And even more crushing is when participants cite the world's mantra, "If you haven't forgotten, then you haven't forgiven." Nothing could be further from the truth, but believers have bought into that fallacy.

The way God has shaped our minds' capacities makes forgetting nearly impossible. Yes, we forget some things, like names, keys, directions, facts on a school test, appointments, etc., but these are more an interruption of our retrieval process rather than outright forgetting. In my view, God has made it impossible to forget what we have seen, heard, and done so that we could never forget God! It gives me great joy to know that once we learn of God, because of the quality and capacities of our God-given minds, it remains impossible for us to forget God. My mind cannot cast out anything, because the harder I try to forget something, the more I remember it. Forgiving, then, is not a function of the mind but of the human will. We must choose to let go of the pain that others have wreaked in our lives or, possibly, that we have brought upon ourselves. And in that process of releasing, we become free of hatred, contempt, and emotional baggage, and free to no longer be stuck in the past but to embrace a new future.

Clinical psychologist Everett Worthington Jr. explains the difference between emotional and decisional forgiveness. He asserts that the forgiveness of which Jesus speaks is decisional forgiveness. In other words, such forgiveness is an active choice we make to turn from the hurts of our past to a healed present and future. I often share the Michael Jackson moonwalk as a metaphor for our choosing not to forgive. It's a fantastic dance that Jackson often performed and is wonderful to watch. However, it's a destructive way to live—facing the past while backing into the future!

Worthington has authored nearly forty books about forgiveness and reconciliation. He believes that "failures in humility seem [to be] at the core of church conflict."[6] No doubt the same failure in humility informs conflict in our communities as well. Church members may say, "[I] can see offenders as having a very different type of spiritual relationship with God than I do. Thus, it is harder for me to forgive."[7] Worthington had to forgive the man who robbed their home and killed his mother while he was in Europe, which he recounts in his writings. It was terribly difficult for him to forgive. He encourages us to "develop the qualities needed for healing. In the same way that empathy, understanding, and valuing stand the best chance of preventing conflict, those same qualities are most likely to heal the wounds that arise from power struggles and unkind acts in congregations."[8] He adds that "forgiveness and reconciliation need to be promoted and practiced. Repeated interaction with like-minded and different-minded believers must be aimed at."[9]

We Christians pray to forgive others as we have been forgiven. Living into this prayer is essential for healthy relationships in our lives at the personal, church, and community levels.

Forgiveness Opens the Doors to Reconciliation

God demonstrated through Job and his friends that God is the only being with real power. We see this in the reconciliation between Job and his friends that followed their forgiveness. I interpret this to mean that forgiveness is an inherent aspect of the sacrifices required of us by God. Job and his friends had wrestled with God and with each other, but we learn through this story that our irreverent wrestling with one another ends when we finally see God as Job did.

I have had many struggles with the need to forgive that have impacted virtually every area of my life including within the church—with friends, family members, colleagues, and neighbors. However, the need to forgive intensified after being tapped at age 11 as one of the first children to integrate the Richmond, Virginia, public schools. From that date on, I can claim sixty-eight years of involvement in racial reconciliation work, including nearly twenty years of professional work in that field. The challenge to forgive was real and initially difficult but the more I grew in my faith, the easier forgiving became. Then and now, folks remain entrenched in such racialized beliefs, justifying slavery by declaring, "Well, slavery is in the Bible!" Reading it superficially might lead to that conclusion. However, the Bible is quite clear, from Genesis to Revelation, that the Holy Writ describes only two ways enslavement is possible: (1) you were captured in war, or (2) you were too poor to provide for yourself. Neither involved the color of a person's skin—the version of slavery that grew out of colonization. So, how do we reseed the very ground of America's historically racialized relationships for the purpose of reconciliation in Christ? Many try but fail because they oversimplify the issues. Multilevel problems cannot be solved with single-level solutions. The collective wounds inflicted by racism are deep but can be healed. However, the healing we long for is delayed or merely superficial without both our individual and collective ability to lament.

Some might declare, "Paul sent that slave back to his owner and slave master," with a sense of validating racialized attitudes. But Scripture declares that Paul did not send Onesimus back as a slave (Philemon 1:10–16). Paul discipled him and saw in him the quality of spirit that later ushered him into becoming one of the church's first bishops. Paul said to Philemon:

> Perhaps the reason he was separated from you for a little while was that you might have him back forever—no longer as a slave, but better than a slave, as a dear brother. He is very dear to me but even dearer to you, both as a fellow man and as a brother in the Lord.
>
> So, if you consider me a partner, welcome him as you would welcome me. If he has done you any wrong or owes you anything, charge it to me. (Philemon 15-18)

Beyond race, much more is broken in church relationships and our world. We are called to reclaim and repair those broken places. N. T. Wright focuses on seven such realities, which he describes as "signposts" that indicate how we are to understand the way the world is and the challenge of being human within it. These signposts help us make sense of the world and our relationships within it, but they all let us down. Therefore, they are broken signposts: justice, love, spirituality, beauty, freedom, truth, and power. Wright says, "First, the universal human longings for these things are all genuine signposts to the fact that we humans are made by a good and wise creator. But each one of them is broken. Indeed, the cross, with all the irony and horror that attaches to it, is to be seen itself as the ultimate broken signpost."[10] These signposts transcend culture and represent the human quest that God graciously placed within us as a reflection of Godself. They point us in the direction for greater well-being and shape our private world. The signposts lend order to any society and culture. Wright continues, "By the power of the spirit of Jesus the Messiah, crucified and risen from the dead, they can become genuine signposts, mended signals, missional marker posts. They will point even more clearly, in the mercy of God, to the cross of Jesus and to his resurrection."[11]

Wright's signposts can guide us as individuals and in the church toward our ability to lament with the goal of repentance. When we mend our broken ways within the church, we will set our path toward reconciliation. From reconciliation, we can assure mature faith and greater church fidelity, and can build stronger communities.

Reconciliation Empowers Community

But how do we get there from here? Any congregation can eventually birth a sense of community, internally and externally, starting with lament. The spice of humility can season any effort that might be offered to others in building a new sense of community. Wright comments, "Confession propels the community to imagine a world beyond their current state of sinful existence. Lament that recognizes the reality of brokenness allows the community to express confession in its proper context. Confession acknowledges the need for God and opens the door for God's intervention. Confession in lament relies on God's work for redemption."[12]

The glorious work and blessings of community, which are gifts from God, are ours to have if we learn to reconcile with one another over the brokenness of the past. Here are a few thoughts that have emerged from my seasons of work on the possibilities for community. I envision a sense of community that is

- can be launched from a common beginning, no matter when or where that might be;
- grants us the privilege to discover or create unity with others;
- is rooted in what we make common among us, not just in what we might have in common.

Choose your community (or communities) wisely, because you either become what it is or it becomes who you are. The best of who we are and what we can be is found within community.

The pandemic showed us that many people exist without a sense of community. The solitude and isolation of that time crushed many folks. Solitude without community is painful, even debilitating, while solitude within community can even be joyous. We are communal beings by nature, which is God's plan for creation. We cannot insist on assimilation, integration, or pro-conciliation without bridging the deeper spiritual divides that color our culture and heighten our racial differences. We know that both whites and blacks have different religious experiences, and we understand that Christianity is not just a well-organized system of truth, but inherent within it is the demand that we live those truths—that we live what we say we believe and what Christ has called us to be.

All Good Things We Have in Christ

As we finish this literary journey together, I want to share a single verse from the New Testament Book of Philemon. In this verse, Paul not only expressed his joy and jubilation over the church that met in Philemon's home, but he also shared his aspiration for them: "I am praying that you will put into action the generosity that comes from your faith as you understand and experience all the good things we have in Christ" (Philemon 6, NLT).

Yes, all the good things we have in Christ! We must continually remind ourselves of this fact, and this is what we share with others: every good thing we have in Christ. However, our history is quite clear that the sharing of our faith has often been lackadaisical, weak, and ineffective. We struggle because we have weighed in on our differences rather than every good thing that is in us for the sake of Christ: our beautiful humanity, our common need for repentance, and our power to forgive and love.

Paul was wondrously creating spiritual infrastructure for Philemon, Onesimus, and the sainted folk who worshipped together, not just in his house, but within a web of Christian mutuality. Faith must be shared, but it must be shared effectively and buttressed by every good thing Christ our Savior has put in us. It should not be marred by the shallow, skin-deep level of humanity that culture often forces upon us. Such cultural prohibitions and inhibitions limit us, taint us, and potentially even restructure the faith we share.

The Church: From Tried to Triumphant

Like Job, we face trials and challenges throughout our lives, both as individuals and as a church community. Some of these trials are of our own making; others happen for reasons beyond our comprehension or control. But as we have witnessed, we have the opportunity to use these challenges to seek a deeper relationship with God and with one another. When we take a Job-like journey, we can arrive at a deeply profound faith and find opportunities for reconciliation. What action steps do you now envision in your Christian faith because of studying Job? Will you make lament a part of your regular prayer life? How will you support others who are falling on hard times? If we choose to follow the path that

Job's faith took and learn from the mistakes of Job's friends, the church will find a healthier path of community for this century and beyond.

Thank you for journeying with me through the Book of Job. I hope that you, like me, have found inspiration and encouragement for finding God amid suffering and have discovered the power of lament in reshaping your life. In closing, I offer one final set of questions for reflection.

Questions for Reflection and/or Response

1. Write, "Teach me, and I will keep quiet; show me what I have done wrong" (6:24). Job pours out his deep anguish about what has happened to him to the point of wishing he had never been born. Has any unexpected tragedy in your life ever brought you to a similar level of despair or grief? Start with, "Oh, my God," then write a lament about it here and share it with others in your group.
2. A lament is not just any verbalized complaint; it is rather a verbal "explosion" of one's hurt, disappointment, regret, or emotional turmoil that one voices in an attitude of sorrow, regret, or even repentance. What do you think is the most essential part of a lament?
3. To me trust is the most important aspect of a community. With it, anything can be achieved; without it, nothing can! All other good elements that comprise any community find their roots in the presence and quality of that trust. Would you agree with my assessment? Why or why not?
4. Make a short list of all our good things in Christ Jesus.
5. Which of the "broken signposts" need to be strengthened in your life?

Notes

1. 1. Gregory A. Smith, "About Three-in-Ten U.S. Adults Are Now Religiously Unaffiliated," Pew Research Center, December 14, 2021, https://www.pewresearch.org/religion/2021/12/14/about-three-in-ten-u-s-adults-are-now-religiously-unaffiliated/.
2. Martin Luther King Jr., "Interview on *Meet the Press*," Stanford: The Martin Luther King, Jr. Research and Education Institute, April 17, 1960, https://kinginstitute.stanford.edu/king-papers/documents/interview-meet-press.
3. Soong-Chan Rah, *Prophetic Lament: A Call for Justice in Troubled Times* (Downers Grove, IL: InterVarsity, 2015), 21.
4. Ibid., 131.
5. Dr. Tesia Mallory, "Litany of Prayer and Lament," https://firebrandmag.com, (2022), https://go.united.edu/webmail/921423/179268286/386b96055c5b107e16bf05fea33d402e6658a7921342f200432537ede1262a96.
6. Everett L. Worthington Jr., *A Just Forgiveness: Responsible Healing without Excusing Injustice* (Downers Grove, IL: InterVarsity, 2009), 149.
7. Ibid., 157.
8. Ibid., 162.
9. Ibid., 165.
10. N. T. Wright, *Broken Signposts: How Christianity Makes Sense of the World* (New York: HarperOne, 2020), 189.
11. Ibid, 191.
12. Ibid.